The Religious Education
of Preschool Children

The Religious Education of Preschool Children

LUCIE W. BARBER

Religious Education Press
Birmingham, Alabama

Library of Congress Cataloging in Publication Data

Barber, Lucie W
    The religious education of preschool children.

    Bibliography: p.
    Includes index.
    1. Christian education of preschool children.
I. Title.
BV1475.7.B36   268'.432   80-27623
ISBN 0-89135-026-8

Religious Education Press, Inc.
1531 Wellington Road
Birmingham, Alabama 35209
10 9 8 7 6 5 4 3

Religious Education Press publishes books exclusively in religious
education and in areas closely related to religious education. It is committed to enhancing and professionalizing religious education through
the publication of serious, significant, and scholarly works.

PUBLISHER TO THE PROFESSION

To All Religious Educators

Contents

Preface

When I reread this book after its completion, I have to admit that the question I asked myself was: "What do you think you are doing with religious education?" I do not plan to answer that question here. Readers must find their own answers from what I have written. I am sure that some religious educators will feel encouraged, while some will feel appalled; some religious educators will applaud, but some will hiss and growl. I can only say that I followed my instincts as a researcher must. I must state that what I have written in the early chapters represents my interpretation of research evidence, while that which appears in the later chapters represents my honest conclusions based upon my knowledge and my experience. I have arrived at my judgments and beliefs because I did not start out as a religious educator.

If you were a religious educator who decided to change your professional allegiance from religious education to psychology, I daresay you would add a needed dimension to psychology. You would have some fresh ideas to enliven the psychologist's discipline. I have gone the reverse route from research psychologist to religious educator. "Enliven" may be too daring a term for my change, but perhaps I can add some new thoughts. We need fresh ideas no matter what the professional discipline. Creativity is the creation of new ideas, but it is also the recombination of old ideas. The recombination of old ideas is what an inter-disciplinary approach can offer. That is the message I hope to bring to religious education.

My antennas tell me that religious educators are ready and anxious for the benefits which can accrue when they pay attention to psychologists, particularly developmental psychologists. I would place in this group the following persons known to me personally: Iris Cully, John Elias, John Hiltz, Bill Koppe, Larry Losoncy, Louise Marie Skoch, Clarence Snelling, Connie Tarasar, Andy Thompson, and Mary Wilcox. There are other personal friends who appreciate developmental psychology: Kendig Cully, Gloria Durka, Dick Gladden, Maria Harris, Marvin Johnson, Chuck Melchert, Gabe Moran, Ellis Nelson, Mary Perkins Ryan, Del Shultz, Joanmarie Smith, David Steward, Mert Strommen, Margaret Thomas, Norma Thompson, and John Westerhoff, plus a host of others who accepted me as I crossed professional lines and asked acceptance in religious education.

They accepted me as a friend. They bore with me during the years of my initiation into religious education. Believe me, the initiation of a research psychologist entering religious education is fraught with difficulties. I had questions which bordered on heresy for some. I had questions which seemed trivial to others. We have survived ten years of mutual irritation. I believe my friends bore with me because of their capacity for Christian love. Now, finally, I believe I can be of help to religious education. I love my religious educator friends and, therefore, I dedicate this book to them. Perhaps they can accept me as a religious educator with them.

One religious educator is of particular importance to me. I thank my husband, John H. Peatling. I have to say that very probably our mutual friends bore with me because of him. If friends have been loving and patient, John has been so seven days a week. This book would never have been written without his support and encouragement.

Finally, I am grateful to the Union College Character Research Project (CRP). Any fresh ideas I can generate come largely because of my training and experience at CRP. The productivity of the founder, Ernest M. Ligon, and his co-workers during the middle decades of the 1900s was inspiring. I must take responsibility for what I have done with that inspiration. Admittedly, I have not followed CRP research curriculum guidelines legalistically. I have reorganized conceptual categories based on current basic research. I have translated CRP terminologies into more current terms. Nonetheless, whatever I have done has been an attempt to make the research of the preceding decades relevant to today. In addition, I have gone on beyond CRP and have added my own conceptualizations throughout the book.

LUCIE W. BARBER
Schenectady, New York

Chapter 1

The Headwaters

When a religious educator seriously considers the question, "What is religious education?" it helps to go back to beginnings. Consider, if you will, infancy and very early childhood. How does religious education begin? Beginnings are supposedly small and simple compared to the complexities encountered along the way. The headwaters of a river are not the deep and turbulent waters one finds midstream or at the mouth of the river. A great deal can be learned about rivers by studying headwaters if the learner keeps in mind that ultimately it is rivers that are being studied. And so it is with religious education if religious educators will try a new orientation to the question, "What is religious education?" Study how religious education begins in infancy and very early childhood. But, at the same time, keep in mind the ultimate goal of religious education. The ultimate goal is fully mature, religious persons.[1]

When you consider religious education in infancy and in very early childhood, one of the first distinctions that must be faced is the difference between religious education and religious training. You can give little children religious training, but it will have little meaning to them intellectually. They can learn Bible stories, Bible verses and prayers, and you can apply all the most up-to-date learning theories to teach them. But, I repeat, it will have little meaning to them intellectually. Religious training in this

5

sense is not appropriate in the religious education of pre-schoolers. Whether you want a Piagetian explanation that the little ones are preoperational or a Goldman explanation that they are prereligious, it amounts to the same thing. Cognitive development has not proceeded to the point where religious content can be handled.

Thus, I am not talking about religious training for little children, although it has its place and will be covered later. I am talking about religious education, that broader term which subsumes religious training. Religious educators are responsible for the whole child, not just the intellectual child. As you learn about the whole river by your study of the headwaters, so you will learn about religious education from your study of beginnings and you will realize that intellectual skills will be found a good distance downstream. What can be seen at the headwaters of religious education, where the waters are shallow and the religious educator's task should be clear? Piaget has named a sensorimotor stage of cognitive development. By sensorimotor Piaget means that cognitive development depends upon a person-environment interaction which can only take place through sensory or motor means. The infant can see, taste, feel, touch, and hear. The infant can also move bodily. These are the only avenues the infant has for interacting with the environment. And it is these interactions which are essential to cognitive growth for the infant. As children pass from the sensorimotor stage to the so-called preoperational stage of cognition in the pre-school years, they are still at the headwaters where the task for religious educators is relatively clear. Preoperational thought has little meaning to adults, although adults themselves went through the stage in childhood. Adults think either concretely or abstractly. In other words, adults think with some degree of logic. Preschoolers cannot think logically or operationally. Education at the preschool level, religious or otherwise, can only be conceived of in preoperational terms. Preschoolers have no capacity for logic. Preschoolers are preoperational or prereligious. That does not mean that they are outside the bounds of religious education, as many religious educators have concluded from Ron Goldman's findings.[2] It is clear that education for infants and preschoolers must differ from education for elementary school and secondary school learners. The point at which sensorimotor interactions occur with the environment is the area where religious educators must begin with infants. In fact, sensorimotor interactions with the environment are important throughout the preschool period.

Inevitably, when I speak of sensorimotor interactions, I speak of sensory feelings. However, most people translate all feelings into emotions and emotionality. However, caution at this point is advisable. In the first place, babies are not born with a full array of emotions.[3] Newborn infants are born with an undifferentiated emotion of excitement. At approximately three months of age, distress and delight are differentiated. The emotional development of two-year-old children probably proceeds to the differentiation of fear, disgust, anger, jealousy, distress, excitement, delight, joy, elation, affection for adults, and affection for children. Shame, anxiety, disappointment, envy, and hope are additionally differentiated by five years of age. The emotions of children differ from the emotions of adults. Children's emotions are more on the surface—intense, uncontrollable, and spontaneous. In fact, most responses of young children are emotional in nature and, thus, must be dealt with in any educational endeavor, once emotional development is appreciated (e.g., do not expect a three-year-old to feel shame, anxiety, disappointment, envy, or hope). There is a second point worth making about emotionality in little children. As children interact with the environment, what you observe is often emotional behavior, but what is also happening for the children is cognitive growth. Sensorimotor interaction is the vehicle children use to attain gradually the cognitive schemata necessary for concrete operational functioning. Cognitive growth is important to remember. The only way children develop cognitively is through interactions with the environment. Although the educator appears to be dealing mainly with emotions and emotional behavior, the child is quietly progressing in cognitive development. It is, of course, artificial to speak about cognitive development, emotional development, or psychomotor development as if each were a separate domain.[4] Each area of development contributes to development in the other areas. A dynamic interaction occurs continuously. The educator needs to keep these complexities in mind. A two-and-a-half year old child attempting to put a puzzle together may scream in frustration that "the pieces are no good." That child's teacher makes a mistake if he or she thinks only of a lesson in controlling emotions. The child is learning a lesson about motor skills (psychomotor), a lesson about cause and effect (cognitive), and an emotionality lesson (affective).

Attitude education necessarily combines the cognitive, the affective, and the psychomotor domains because attitudes, according to Rokeach, are organizations of interrelated beliefs, "with each belief having cognitive, affective, and behavioral components."[5] Religious educators inevitably are concerned with beliefs. The contention that beliefs have cognitive, affective, and behavioral components may help clarify the educator's task. An attitude, with its belief structure, is not just cognitive, not just affective, nor is it just an energizer of behavior. It is an intricate combination. Thus, religious attitude education involves cognitive goals and affective goals and behavioral goals. The educator does not talk solely about knowledge attainment or acceptable emotional control or development of motor and perceptual abilities. All three in concert are involved. Krathwohl and Bloom list attitudes in the affective domain under the most complex category of educational goals. That affective category is valuing. Attitudes are not mentioned in the cognitive domain or in the psychomotor domain of educational goals. The influence of these taxonomy monographs has been considerable in both education and psychology. I believe this influence is at least one reason why many educators assume that attitudes are purely affective. However, the authors of those taxonomies are careful to point out the overlap of the three domains. Their aim in separating the domains artificially is to assist educators methodologically. Another aspect to keep in mind is that the taxonomies of educational objectives list outcomes of education. A categorization of outcomes is helpful in evaluating the product of teaching. Such a categorization is also helpful in systematizing the anticipation of teaching. Yet it says little about the whys and the hows for obtaining an outcome. I contend that more assistance in the whys (theory) and the hows (application) in attitude education comes from Milton Rokeach. His book, *The Open and Closed Mind,* threw him into the limelight in attitude research.[6] Then his work became more definitive and more structural in *Beliefs, Attitudes, and Values.* Beliefs are structured by attitudes which in turn are structured by values. It is Rokeach's contention that beliefs have cognitive, affective, and behavioral components which are of interest to attitude educators. Attitude educators' interest in beliefs is ensured by Rokeach's further rationale that attitudes are made up of at least two or more beliefs. Also of interest is his statement that two or more attitudes contributing to an attitude system can comprise a religious ideology. This is of greater interest to religious educators. In *Beliefs, Attitudes, and Values,* Rokeach concludes with an affirmation for the rationale that values are the overarching area to be researched. This is interesting because the taxonomists of educational goals reached the conclusion that valuing is a necessary category for educational outcomes. Rokeach's later publication, *The Nature of Human Values,* carries his views further on the centrality of values in human affairs.[7] The amount of data produced by his theory is massive. Much of the data is of interest to religious educators, but only tangentially. Yet his placing emphasis on values is paramount. All religious educators are involved with values.

In a way, I would like to substitute the term "attitude education" for "values education." Unfortunately, values education is often associated with values clarification.[8] I wish to avoid confusing attitude education with values clarification. I am not too sanguine about values clarification because the theoretical underpinnings are too relativistic. Theoretically, it seems to me that religious educators have a more solid base. Religious educators, because they are religious, are committed to certain values which describe their faith.

Thus, I have chosen the term *attitude education* for the religious education of the young child. I do this for two reasons: (1) as I define attitude education, attention is maintained on cognitive components, and (2) attitudes are value-laden with cognitive, affective, and behavioral components.

I am trying to make religious education clear at the preschool level. That is not the same as saying that I am trying to make it simple. Religious education or any education at any level is far from simple. By using the term attitude education I am attempting to draw your attention to cognitive plus affective plus behavioral aspects. Let me go a step further. When you deal with preschool children, you are aware of behavior because most preschoolers are active. Their energy amazes me. You are also aware of emotions. Emotions are readily apparent with preschoolers because their emotions tend to be so off-the-cuff, so uncontrollably random.

You are less aware of cognition with preschoolers. The signs of comprehension are very misleading when you recognize that adults no longer remember what preoperational thinking is all about. Behavior and emotionality are observed. These are clear. Yet the term attitude education can alert the observer to the fact that cognitive growth is occurring. I believe that educators should recognize the importance of cognitive, affective, and psychomotor development. Yet during the preschool years (the preoperational period) emotions and overt behavior must be dealt with. Teachers deal with sensory feelings and gradually differentiating emotions, and they deal with psychomotor abilities. There is a cognitive involvement, as you will perceive when I state educational goals for specific attitudes in later chapters. Yet the educational approach is through behavior and feelings. Behavior and feelings are the means but not the ends in attitude education.

I would like to make one further point here before you continue reading this book. You will totally misunderstand what I am trying to accomplish if you enter the remaining text with the thought that I am outlining either (1) affective education (how to teach children how to use their emotionality constructively) or (2) discipline methodologies (how to make children submit to adult norms for behavior). My aim is much more general and, I would maintain, much more deeply Christian. Christ came to give us life—cognitive life, affective life, and behavioral life in its fullest. I promote attitude education for preschoolers in the tripart sense for religious educators. Certainly I will talk about emotionality and discipline. However, those are means to a more general goal—the learning of foundational attitudes.

In conclusion: I have declared that religious education for children before the formal school years is attitude education. The attitudes which preschoolers can learn are precursors to the mature attitudes of fully developed, religious persons. I have not said that attitude education *equals* religious education for all persons, only for preschool children. Religious education on beyond the preschool years is not my concern here, and I do not want to declare attitude education and religious education as equivalents for all age levels. However, I am convinced that the approach of attitude education during the preschool years can be refreshing and helpful for religious educators who are searching for ways to minister to little children.

Chapter 2

Parents as Paraprofessionals

Religious educators have somehow survived a good bit of criticism, constructive and otherwise. Unfortunately, not very many have heeded repeated calls for reform. In 1967 both Ellis Nelson and Gabriel Moran pleaded for more attention to the education of parents of very young children.[1] John Westerhoff repeated the challenge in 1970,[2] and in 1973 James Michael Lee took up the gauntlet.[3] Lee emphasizes "the importance of the family as the primary agent of religious instruction." Lee has adequately reviewed the research on the importance of the preschool years and stresses that "early family life and background constitute the most powerful, the most pervasive, and the most perduring variable affecting virtually all phases of an individual's learning." Something of extreme importance to religious education is happening in families. Responsible religious educators should be engaged in parent education. The difficulty, however, stems from the general lack of information which tells religious educators exactly what to do. Religious educators must rearrange their priorities to include teaching parents how to become paraprofessional religious educators of their infants and preschool children. They must teach parents the specifics of attitude education. This particular ministry can be carried out effectively through the use of this book and other available materials.[4]

13

Religious educators must be challenged to develop teams of paraprofessional parents in every parish. Unless professionals train parents as the religious educators of their young children, they (the professionals) are throwing aside a responsibility which is theirs. Religious educators must pay attention to the headwaters, the babies, if they are to affect the rest of the river and realize that mature Christians are their ultimate goal. They must step out systematically to prepare parents to teach Christian attitudes in the home. Unless parents are prepared for their role as paraprofessionals, the church runs the risk of the further decline of its influence in the lives of people.

In terms of meeting the challenge to educate parents, you can begin by turning your attention to the several factors that play to your advantage.

1. Parents essentially want the best for their children. They want their children to have all the good things they had as children, but they are inspired to give their children even better things. For Christian parents this means even better religious education than they received. Parents are eager to improve their children's religious education.

2. Parenthood, the act of giving birth to another human being, provides a "teachable moment." Parents are ripe for learning. If you have observed a group of young parents, you no doubt know that conversation about their babies is inevitable. That interchange can be looked upon as group learning. However, the learning can be systematized.

3. Parents are the natural teachers of their children. From the moment an infant is born, the education of the child has begun. Unfortunately, parents do not recog-

nize the fact that they are teachers or, if they do, they recognize only their responsibility to teach eating skills, bathroom skills, and dressing skills. Many parents fail to realize that they are teachers of attitudes.

4. Parents are in physical contact with their children more consistently than anyone else in the world. Working parents may not spend all day with their children, but there is a regularity of contact which can have a positive, cumulative effect.

5. Parents are better acquainted with their children than anyone else. They are ego-involved with their offspring, and the intimacy of the relationship provides a marvelous learning environment.

6. Parents recognize their child's uniqueness. This means that teaching-learning can be on a one-to-one basis. Individualized instruction, so difficult to achieve in a classroom with thirty children and one teacher, can be achieved easily in the home.

If these advantageous factors about parents can be used in plans for ministering to them, meeting the challenge of parent education will be more manageable.

If I sound confident about meeting the challenge of teaching parents to be paraprofessionals in the religious education of their little children, I have reason to be. Attitude education and parent assistance have been my areas of study for over fifteen years. I know a little about it, enough to want to write this book. My professional position is Director of Applied Research at the Union College Character Research Project (CRP). CRP has been involved in religious attitude education longer than any other institution in this country. CRP has produced and tested curricular materials for all age levels. For the past twelve years, CRP has concentrated on materials for parents of infants and preschool children (see Appendix B). There is a book for parents of children from birth to thirty months. Another book covers the second year of life more specifically. There is also a field-tested, parenting skills program for parish groups of parents of preschoolers, and seven books related to that program are in production. I am fortunate to have had the experience and training afforded me by my association with the Character Research Project.

In what follows I will share with you how, in general, parents can teach attitudes to their little children. The specifics will come later.

Chapter 3

Teaching Attitudes

An attitude is defined as "an enduring, learned predisposition to behave in a consistent way toward a given class of objects."[1] For religious attitudes then, the given class of objects are religious in nature. I will be talking about the general religious attitudes of faith, hope, and love. Can little children be taught to have attitudes of faith, hope, and love? Of course not, not in the sense that those attitudes are held by mature Christians. Yet little children can learn some basic outlooks on life which are foundations for their future, mature attitudes. Unless they acquire these foundational outlooks before school age, they may have difficulty learning to have faith, hope and love later on in their lives.[2]

There is not much difficulty in recognizing that the parent who is cuddling a baby and lovingly looking after that baby's needs is somehow or other teaching faith, hope, and love to that child. It is that "somehow or other" which must be defined and ordered for parents. How is attitude education accomplished? That question needs a general answer before we can take the next step which is showing parents specifically how to be paraprofessionals in the religious education of their children.

In *The Flow of Religious Instruction,*[3] James Michael Lee made four helpful points: (1) ". . . The teacher should consciously and deliberately teach for attitudes." Parents must be helped to be aware of the importance of teaching attitudes and then consciously and deliberately go about the task.

(2) "... The teacher should put the student in a learning situation which is concrete and which contains many firsthand experiential variables." This admonition is extremely important with preschool, preoperational children. At this level of development, learning occurs only by direct encounters with the environment. The child must touch, hear, see, smell, and taste. The child must manipulate and experience in order to learn.

(3) "... The teacher should so structure the concrete learning situation that it features considerable interpersonal interaction ...." The child, in order to gain the basic outlooks which are the foundations for faith, hope, and love, must interact with others. Infants in institutions isolated from human contact become retarded and unhealthy.[4]

(4) "... All the variables in the total education environment must be deliberately targeted toward the learning of values." Translated for parents this admonition involves structuring the home and family members in ways that will reinforce desired values.

The four points are general principles and are very important in attitude education. However, they are still very general. I can be much more specific, particularly at the preschool level. Religious education for young children is relatively clear because it is solely attitude education. You do not have to be bothered with teaching facts or skills except as they may contribute to the learning of attitudes. Your entire focus is religious attitudes or that part of religious attitudes that preschool children can learn. And that part of religious attitudes is relatively small and definable.

Before defining the crucial area of religious attitudes that can be taught to young children, it will prove helpful to present for consideration some further principles in attitude education. They are more specific than the very general principles already discussed, but not yet as specific as the actual techniques which you will find in the next few chapters. As you, the religious educator, minister to parents of young children, these are the points to emphasize.

First, the single, most powerful teaching method with preschoolers is *reinforcement*. Certainly, I am talking about conditioning. However, I am not speaking about classical conditioning. I refer to operant conditioning. The teacher positively reinforces desired behaviors. If you are uncomfortable with B. F. Skinner,[5] consider this. There is no other way to teach an infant. You cannot preach to, lecture at, reason with, or explain to an infant, at least not with any discernible good effects. Operant conditioning is your only resource. Remember, too, that conditioning occurs whether or not one is aware of it. The two-month-old baby smiles. The parent is delighted and reinforces the behavior by demonstrating that delight. And, in this way, one of the first social learning experiences of the infant is begun. Physical objects are reinforcing too. Stop and think about the reinforcement that a pacifier, a security blanket, or food provide. The power of operant conditioning in the preschool years cannot be escaped. On the other hand, as a responsible religious educator, you can understand and contain conditioning so that its use can be devoted to the release of human potential. With the religious goals of faith, hope, and love brought to the forefront, you can march confidently toward the learner's freedom and dignity. However, the only way to begin the march is with conditioning. One last word on this subject lest you are still leery of a Skinnerian box or a Walden II. There are two types of reinforcement, positive and adversive. You can rely heavily on positive reinforcement. It is not possible to eliminate adversive reinforcement in the practical, everyday, human world. Parents do lose their tempers. Toddlers do dart out into the street. Yet, for the most part, the most effective teaching is achieved by positive reinforcement.

Positive reinforcement exists in the form of any action of the teacher that encourages the learner to repeat a behavior. It can be a hug, a smile, a kiss, a star on a chart, or a piece of candy. This leads to a second principle in attitude education. What reinforces Jennifer does not necessarily reinforce Eddie. The principle which parents need to deal with is that every child is *unique*.[6] It is not difficult to convince parents that their child is different from any other child (although they might think "better," not "different"). Recognizing a child's uniqueness is important because it leads squarely into a third principle.

Parents as teachers should become *researchers* of their child. How else are they to determine what kind of reinforcement works with their unique child? Perhaps "researcher" is too strong a word. I like it because I am a researcher. I use the word to point out the importance of observation and evaluation. The teacher observes and then evaluates the result. If the result is not the desired result, then a revision is necessary and the cycle starts again until success is achieved. This researching is necessary for determining reinforcements, but it is also necessary for assessing level of development.

The fourth principle is that parents must be able to *assess* their child's level of maturity in the particular attitude involved. For example, if the attitude is generosity, it is unrealistic to expect a child to share a toy until that child has matured to the point of appreciating the concept of possession. One-year-old babies have no idea that objects belong to different people. They will grab anything they can get their hands on. Two-year-old toddlers are just beginning to differentiate between what is theirs and what belongs to someone else. You can force a two-year-old to share, but that is hardly conducive to teaching generosity. Attitude education is effective only with knowledge of level of maturity. Such knowledge depends upon assessment. I will be speaking about levels and assessment constantly.

One reason for assessment is that attitude education proceeds *one step at a time.* That is the fifth principle. The parent must assess the child's level of maturity in order to determine how to proceed to just the next level. This is realistic and removes the burden from both parent and child of expecting too much. Unduly high expectations are behind many an educational failure. Do not expect more of the learner than is realistic. Proceed one step at a time.

Goal setting is the sixth principle. Once parents have appreciated the level of maturity of their child and have recognized the next step that is realistic, they should set a goal. The goal is a behavioral objective related to the attitude being taught. A goal specifies a behavior which, when it occurs, can be reinforced. Goals are set by parents with very young children. But four-and-five-year-old children can have a beneficial part in goal setting.

A further principle addresses the way in which a parent-teacher can elicit the behavior for which a goal was set. Parent-teachers *provide a stimulus.* That is an elegant way of saying that the parent-teacher tells a story, acts out the behavior, arranges for friends to visit, puts a poster on the refrigerator door, or whatever might elicit a particular behavior. Providing a stimulus takes me back to uniqueness and researching, of course. What stimulates one child may not stimulate another. Parent-teachers must research their own child in order to see what stimulates a goal behavior.

One last principle of demonstrated effectiveness in attitude education remains. *Build on strengths.* Too many educators believe their job is to correct weaknesses. They start with the question, "What's wrong with this child?" I am suggesting that educators and, in particular, religious educators should start with the question, "What's right with this child?" This cycles back to positive reinforcement and points to a further insight. The entire positive approach is important in attitude education because the strong message perceived by the child is, "I have strengths. I am a person of worth." The child then becomes an eager learner. Learners learn only that which they are willing to learn.

The eight principles of attitude education are, of course, interrelated. Each is incomplete without the others. I have not said all that there is to be said about attitude education, but important groundwork has been laid. In the next chapters, I will start building on that groundwork. As I move on to discuss the specific religious attitudes of faith, hope, and love, the importance of the eight underlying principles will unfold.

There remain faith, hope, and love. Why did I choose these three concepts as a vehicle for demonstrating to you the process of attitude education for young children? I could have chosen the immaculate conception, the virgin birth, and the resurrection. Granted, that would have made my task more difficult; nonetheless, it could have been done. For each of those concepts, the methodology remains the same as the methodology I will attempt to demonstrate with faith, hope, and love.

There are two main reasons why I did not choose the immaculate conception, the virgin birth, and the resurrection. The first reason has to do with my personal ministry. I want to be helpful to religious educators in general. I believe that I have a helpful message to communicate. Thus, I am anxious to communicate to as many as possible. It is of little value to risk arguments about dogma for Christians of various beliefs. Certainly, most can agree on the importance of faith, hope, and love. Religious educators of faiths other than Christian can also resonate to faith, hope, and love. Therefore, my rationale is that in demonstrating a methodology, choose a high level of generality for illustration.

Faith, hope, and love are general enough for all religious educators to accept. You might object to my specificities of the immaculate conception, the virgin birth, and the resurrection. I want to avoid bickering, at least at this stage of the game. What I really want to do is to demonstrate methodology. With faith, hope, and love, I can do that.

There is one other reason why I chose faith, hope, and love. They are all positive concepts. I could have chosen sin, hell, and damnation. They are, psychologically, negative terms. If I am going to be true to my experience and knowledge, I have to say that negative concepts are off limits in the religious education of little children. Religious educators have turned the corner on fire and brimstone, for the most part. A major problem is recovering from that fire and brimstone era.[7]

The potential of religious education today is seen in new lights. At least I hope it is, because otherwise I would not bother with a book on theoretical methodology for attitude education. I hope you can see the potential in terms of faith, hope, and love. Faith, hope, and love are desperately needed in today's world.

Chapter 4

Faith

What does faith mean to you? Christian faith means to me, "Trust in a God creator and the self-confidence to accept God's grace." I am not a theologian. I am a psychologist of early childhood with an interest in religious education. If you will accept my very general definition of faith as "Trust in a God creator and the self-confidence to accept God's grace," then a discussion of how this definition may apply to preschool children is in order.

As a young parent this was a puzzle to me. A creating God and acceptance of grace! I saw no way that such concepts had anything to do with infants and very little children. As I was bringing up my children, I certainly wanted them to have faith. Yes, they went to Sunday School regularly. Yes, I taught Sunday School. Yes, the Barber family was there for every festivity, every church supper, every Sunday School play. In a small parish, a family of seven makes a difference! We did the accepted things at home, too. We prayed as a family. Sunday was a special day. The church calendar was central. What Christmases! What Easters! We did what, at that time, we were supposed to do.

Yet there was a randomness to what went on. We loved, we celebrated, and the result was good. But in terms of responsible religious education for the children, it could have been better.

In 1964, I joined the staff of the Union College Character Research Project (CRP), and there began a long educational process that led me to question some of my earlier parenting and religious education methods. The Character Research Project had systematized religious education, up to a point, for all age levels. They began, at the theological level, by mapping out those attitudes that form the basis of the Christian outlook.[1] From there they traced back, by developmental levels, the beginnings of these attitudes as they are expressed at every age level.[2] For example, returning to the definition of faith, "Trust in a God creator and the self-confidence to accept God's grace," it is clear that the focus is on attitudes: the attitude of trust (in this case with God as the object) and the attitude of self-confidence (with grace as the object).

Now God and grace are very abstract concepts, far too abstract to have meaning to preschoolers. However, foundational attitudes of trust and confidence are not beyond preschoolers. Religious educators can introduce youngsters to more concrete objects: for instance, trust in the dependability of parents who love their children or confidence in the predictability of events.

Thus, CRP mapped out religious attitudes and delineated just what can be accomplished at each age level in laying the basis for fully developed attitudes. This has been an awesome contribution to religious education.[3] It means that you can replace the earlier random approach to educating children with a systematic understanding of (1) what attitudes you want children to learn, (2) what your goals are in teaching these attitudes, and (3) how to go about teaching these attitudes while respecting the capacities of each developmental level.

With that introduction, we can proceed to the "nuts and bolts" of this chapter. How do you go about introducing the foundational attitudes of faith to the infant and young child? When you trace back the mature attitudes of faith to the preschool years, you must realize that any educational goals you may choose are interrelated with the educational goals for hope or love. Thus, the goals I am about to list are not the sum total of the foundational attitudes necessary for faith. Other related goals will be found in chapters 5 and 6.

The first attitude preschool children can learn is to trust the dependability of those who love and care for them. Parents are God to a small child. Trust in the dependability of parents should be encouraged as a precursory attitude to trust in God.

The second attitude is an appreciation of nature. The attributes of nature are a very concrete demonstration of the gift of grace. Little children can learn to enjoy the weather, the seasons, the landscape, and all growing plants and creatures. Genuine appreciation of nature is a precursor for faith in the Creator. Little children can learn a third attitude which is a precursor to mature faith. They can learn to have faith in the predictability of events. This particular attitude may seem irrelevant to you, but it is not to preschool children. A foundation for faith is trust in routine, or, from the perspective of children, learning that the environment is orderly and that events occur when they are expected.

These, then, are three very general educational goals to be dealt with in this chapter. Children can learn to:

1. Trust the dependability of those who love and care for them;
2. Appreciate nature;
3. Have faith in the predictability of events.

These precursory attitudes may seem to be small progress toward trusting in a God creator or having the self-confidence to accept God's grace, but they are essential foundations.

In the rest of this chapter each of the three attitudes will be discussed in such a way as to illustrate certain of the principles introduced in chapter 3. This chapter will give illustrations of Assessment, Progression Step by Step, and Goal Setting. You will recall that there were eight principles. The other five principles will be illustrated in subsequent chapters. Three principles are enough for a beginning.

DEPENDABILITY OF THE CARETAKER

How fortunate to begin with children's trust in the dependability of caretakers (parents)! There is little difficulty recognizing the relationship between the dependent child's faith in parents and the mature Christian's faith in God. Parents are like gods to little children. If the parents are good and loving gods, wholesome attitudes will be formed. If parents are rejecting and domineering, unwholesome attitudes will be formed. I am going to assume that children have loving caretakers in order to move on. What are the levels of development which can be predicted as children develop a trust in the dependability of their caretakers? I am going to list five levels from least mature to most mature for preschoolers. I am going to assign labels to each level to let you know generally where each level is between birth and six years of age. The description of each level is a brief behaviorally-oriented picture of normal children.

1. *Newborn.* Newborn babies are completely dependent upon caretakers. Trust, as such, does not exist. In fact, tiny babies are unaware of persons as entities separate from

self. In such a helpless condition, newborns must have loving support as a foundation for all future development.

2. *Infancy.* Infants gradually learn to recognize parents. Infants express pleasure when needs are met. Although still highly dependent upon caretakers, infants are becoming aware of some distinctions between self, objects and others. Again, loving support from parents is all-important.

3. *Toddlers.* These little children are testing their newly-found independence that comes with mobility and language. While this testing may be trying at times, pleasing their parents is a strong motivator. Family is a cherished haven to these young explorers.

4. *Runabouts.* At this level of development, children can dress themselves, feed themselves, take care of personal hygiene chores, and begin to interact meaningfully with others. The new dimension of interacting with others adds an important aspect to the relationship with parents. They need and ask for their parents' advice, training, and guidance. This is the level when parents are worshiped by their children. Parents are God.

5. *On Beyond.* Children at this level have learned two important lessons about trusting caretakers: (1) parents are not infallible; (2) there are other authority figures upon whom they can depend. As their perspective of the world broadens, they become realistic about whom they can trust. With such a foundation, the possibility of eventually putting their faith in the ultimate caretaker, God, is maximized.

The five levels of development in trusting the dependability of caretakers give you a simple assessment device.

Parents can read these brief descriptions and assign their child to a level. Once they have assessed their child's level of development, parents can look to just the next level and decide upon a realistic goal. Development is a step-by-step process and goals structured by an assessment device help parents to be realistic.

APPRECIATION OF NATURE

Nature and the laws of nature are God's handiwork. Children who can appreciate nature are building foundations for faith in a God creator. The descriptions of the five levels of development from least to most mature for this foundational attitude follow:

1. *Newborn.* Newborn babies enter this world with no appreciation of nature. The ability to appreciate anything is entirely absent because babies are entirely locked in egocentricity, a Piagetian term meaning that perception is wholly self. You and I can think in terms of me, you, a family, a house, the outdoors. Newborns cannot.

2. *Infancy.* Object constancy is achieved. That is another Piagetian term which means that babies now are aware that an object exists even though it cannot be seen. All things considered, that is quite a mental accomplishment. It opens the door for children to perceive God's creation. Object constancy unlocks egocentricity, but the door is still just ajar.

3. *Toddler.* The young explorers venture forth. Everything that can be felt or tasted is fair game: pots, pans, pebbles, or peonies. But the attention span is short and activities are random. There seems to be no rhyme or reason to actions. However, parents have an asset. These children are great

imitators, and parents can use that trait in teaching their children to enjoy nature.

4. *Runabout.* This is a priceless level of maturity. Young children are not only thirsty for knowledge about the environment in which they live, but they will ask endless questions, accept parents' advice and training, and demonstrate persistence in learning tasks. Their capacity to be awed by the beauties of nature is inspiring. But do not be surprised by animism. It is normal at this level of maturity for children to infer that inanimate objects have hearts and souls and behave for their personal gratification. "The sun tells me when to get up." "That chair bumped me."

5. *On Beyond.* Some very mature preschoolers can begin to learn the concrete laws of nature. They can appreciate weather and the seasons. Learning about the laws of nature is very important in a religious sense. The security of experiencing God's orderliness in nature can be a powerful building block for future faith.

Let me illustrate the principles of Assessment, Progression Step-by-Step, and Goal Setting by pretending to be a parent. I have assessed my daughter Christy as belonging to the Toddler level of maturity in appreciation of nature. She is a dynamo of energy but does not stay with any one project for very long. On the other hand, she is a copycat. She will imitate whatever I do. Now, I would like her to take a step, and it has got to be small, toward a level 4 child's awe of beauty. I am ready to set a goal and I want it to be very specific and to involve something that I know Christy can do. My goal with Christy is:

On Thursday morning we will go to the park and visit the gardens. My delight and exclamations over the flowers can be imitated by Christy.

Please take note of that goal. It is specific, naming place and time. A goal is much more likely to be carried out when it is specifically stated. If Christy's mother said to herself, "The next time we see flowers, I will . . .," a next time might never occur. Another mark of a good goal is that the goal setter is able to judge if the goal has or has not been attained. The mother can judge whether or not Christy imitates her behaviors of exclamation and delight.

FAITH IN THE PREDICTABILITY OF EVENTS

Closely related to the outlook of appreciation of nature (which is predictable) is the outlook of faith in the predictability of events. Think of little children as strangers in a brand new world. There is so much to learn about their environment which more experienced adults take for granted. A stranger in a new land hunts for meaning and assurance. The assurance of predictability is a step on the road to faith in a God who orders our lives.

1. *Newborns.* Newborns are completely locked in egocentricity. Self is all there is. Babies are unaware of events and have no sense of time.

2. *Infancy.* Infants gradually learn to be aware of themselves as distinct from objects and others. They can even learn that they have some voice (usually crying) in getting caretakers to attend to their needs. However, they want what they desire right away. Delayed gratification has little or no meaning.

3.*Toddler.* Toddlers can wait short periods of time for their needs to be met. They are busy exploring cause and effect. They throw a ball in order to learn where it will go. They can anticipate a coming event. An outstanding characteristic of this maturity level is a love for routine and orderliness. The bedtime routine may be trying for adults, but if the caretakers try to leave out just one stuffed animal or fail to arrange the covers just so, they will have problems.

4. *Runabouts.* These little children understand a sequence of events. "After rest period you can have some orange juice, and then we will go to the grocery store." They will play-act an anticipated event because they want to be prepared for what comes next. They will practice skills so that they can do things correctly. On the other hand, this is a level where children often have a fantasy world, a kind of buffer zone that offers them security when they encounter problems in the real world. Fantasy is normal and necessary.

5. *On Beyond.* Fantasy play decreases as play becomes more realistic. These mature preschoolers have confidence in the dependability of their environment. They can predict events within a narrow time range. The laws of nature have some meaning. Children with such confidence have an excellent foundation for a future, mature faith in God the Creator.

As another example, Jeffrey's father can illustrate Assessment, Progression Step-by-Step, and Goal Setting. What can he do to help Jeffrey learn about predictability of events? Jeffrey is a newborn baby. As Jeffrey's father looks at the next step, the Infancy level, he decides upon a goal which will help Jeffrey to learn that he can have a voice in getting his parents to attend to his needs.

"When Jeff gives that hunger cry, and I think I know that one now, I will give him a bottle. That way Jeff will have taken a first step in learning that he can depend on us to take care of his needs."

Jeffrey will eventually learn that he can influence the predictability of events. It is one small step which must be repeated continually, but it is a systematic, conscious step in the progression of his attitude education.

Religious educators can assist parents in:

1. Assessing the level of development of their child;
2. Looking for the next step in a step-by-step progression;
3. Setting a goal for achieving a step.

Illustrations of these three principles in attitude education will be repeated in the next two chapters and other principles will be added. The next chapter will explore hope.

Chapter 5

Hope

Hope, in my terms, means two things:

1. Reliance on the kingdom of God now and hereafter;
2. Trust in the potential for obtaining greater knowledge and understanding of the unknown.

Both of these attitudes are heavily laden with a future orientation. Little children, even six-year-olds, have very little sense of the future. However, there are attitudes which can be developed that are important foundations for mature religious hope.

1. *A positive attitude toward life.* This does not preclude acknowledging the worst or the mediocre. It is a realistic optimism.

2. *A joyful attitude toward learning.* This attitude includes an appreciation of creativity, purposiveness, and persistence in learning. With these two general attitudes, little children are well-equipped to face life with hope.

In this chapter, I will go through the levels of development for each of the two general attitudes so that the bases for *assessment* for each are available to you. Then, I will talk about *step-by-step progression* as *goal setting* is illustrated. The importance of *researching* will be introduced so that the uniqueness of the child at a particular level of development is appreciated. Researching the unique child is necessary in goal setting because a good goal must elicit behavior which the parent can then *reinforce*. By the end of this chapter you will have had illustrations of six of the eight principles of effective attitude education.

A POSITIVE APPROACH TO LIFE

There is reason to believe that little children come into this world as optimists. In fact, considering what they have to contend with in the natural course of events, it is amazing how cheerful they can remain. They are misunderstood, abused, barely tolerated, and isolated. And yet so many of them maintain a basic cheerfulness. Is this false bravado? Certainly children learn very early that they must submit to authority. Who else other than adults can they depend upon in living each day? And certainly they want things to be pleasant for themselves in these early years when egocentricity is so prevalent. Even two-year-old children can sense that things are pleasant for them only if the result of their behavior is pleasant for adults.[1]

Nevertheless, there must be a Christian basis for creating a positive approach to life which will help children to recognize the bad and the mediocre and choose the best. I maintain that children must be helped to learn how to deal with two potentially troublesome areas. There are two areas of constant relevance to little children: frustrations and fears.[2] Unless and until children can deal positively with frustrations and fears, there is little likelihood that they can be genuinely cheerful and optimistic. Therefore, in the following assessment device you will find in each description of a developmental level the three elements of (1) dealing with frustrations, (2) coping with fears, and (3) expressing cheerfulness.

1. *Newborn.* Newborns experience the frustrations of physical discomfort and usually express these frustrations by crying. Of course, newborns have no way to cope with frustrations except through reflexive bodily activity. There is a myth that newborn babies fear loud noises or falling.[3] There is no evidence to support this contention or, in fact, the idea that newborns have any fears, if you believe as I do that fears are learned or, at most, are a reaction to that which has not yet been learned. Cheerfulness at this stage of complete egocentricity is dependent upon adults' meeting the baby's physical needs.

2. *Infancy.* Frustrations occur, at least in our culture, when physical activity or actions are confined or limited. Infants become very vocal when denied a fascinating toy or the chance to explore on all fours. Fear can now be recognized by adults. As perception and discriminations mature toward the end of infancy, there are visible signs of fear of strangers: cringing, clinging, and crying. Infants are helpless in controlling emotions of any kind. Self-pleasure is the only pleasure infants appreciate, although they have little understanding of how to achieve self-pleasure.

3. *Toddler.* Delayed gratification which still frustrates toddlers may elicit temper tantrums. The bipolarity of the desire for independence and the need for continuing dependence generates instability and confusion which often are expressed by negativism and rage. Fear of the strange and unfamiliar, fears learned from others, and fears learned from experience are intense. Fears of darkness, animals, and of being left alone are common. Unfortunately, at this stage children have no defenses or coping skills. However, there is one bright light. Toddlers are

beginning to recognize the importance of their parents. Pleasing their parents becomes important to them. They also appreciate the physical comfort their parents give when the toddlers are afraid. They depend on their parents' stability and calm when emotions seethe uncontrollably.

4. *Runabout.* These children have learned that it is normal to have frustrations, that everyone has frustrations. They have also learned that there are constructive ways to deal with frustrations. Fears may be intensified because a new class of fears is now within their capacity: imaginary fears. On the other hand, cognitive structures have developed to the point where the child will seek explanations. Rationales and guidance from parents are actively sought. These children now equate self-pleasure with pleasing their parents. If everyone is cheerful, the rewards to children are greater. This may seem self-centered, but it is a step along the way to the next level.

5. *On Beyond.* At the most mature preschool level, children have learned how to deal with their frustrations with some success. Many of the roles necessary for particular frustrations have become habits. Fears have been put into perspective, although preschoolers do not always employ mature, rational logic in doing so. For example, closing the bogeyman in the drawer is not the rationale of an adult, but it serves children's needs. One big advance at this level has to do with cheerfulness. These children have an optimistic outlook because they are able to concern themselves with the welfare of others. They even go out of their way to help others to be cheerful. That is solid progress.

Such progress can be achieved one step at a time. If a parent assessed a child at level 3, all that can be expected is progress toward level 4. Setting a goal for level 5 is not only unrealistic, it is self-defeating for both parent and child.

Return to Christy's mother who is about to set a goal. How does that mother assess Christy's level of development in gaining a positive approach to life? She reads or talks about the levels. She thinks about what she has observed in Christy's behavior. She recognizes that the dark frightens Christy. She has observed that Christy avoids looking out of the window at night and refuses to sleep without a night light on. Observation is part of *researching*. Her concern for Christy's particular behaviors attests to the mother's concern for her daughter's *uniqueness*. The mother is searching for a goal that will elicit desired behavior which she in turn can *reinforce*. A goal is like an hypothesis. If x, then y. But the y has to be evaluated in order to judge the appropriateness of x. That is *research*. Observe, design a strategy, and then evaluate the results. Research is necessary in order to deal with uniqueness. Uniqueness, in turn, must be considered in order to discover what reinforces a desired behavior most effectively.

This is the goal for Christy assessed at level 3: "I want Christy to learn to cope with her fear of the dark. Tonight I will put my arm around her at bedtime and tell her a story about the friendly darkness. Then I will suggest that we look out of the window together and see whether or not she will respond."

The mother is a researcher. She is setting up an experiment and plans to evaluate the results. If Christy will go to the window with her, she can reinforce that behavior by hugging her or by talking about the sleeping animals or by doing whatever reinforces her unique child. She is en-

gaged in taking one small step at level 3 which will help
Christy make progress, one step at a time, toward level 4.
She provides the physical reassurance to which a level 3
child can respond but also introduces an explanation that a
level 4 child might appreciate. She will research results in
order to determine whether or not reinforcements match
Christy's uniqueness.

THE JOY OF LEARNING

Learning begins at birth. The trouble is that too many
adults choose the definition of learning as "knowledge or
skill gained by instruction or study." Try instructing a baby
and see what results you get. Learning for infants and
preschoolers comes from the child's interactions with the
environment. You may call it play, but the children are
learning. Toddlers who drop bits of food from the high
chair are learning about cause and effect. The two nursery
school children playing in the housekeeping corner are
learning social interaction skills. Adults can hinder a
child's learning by limiting opportunities for interaction,
but they cannot extinguish learning (unless they keep children in complete isolation). Learning comes naturally.
Learning also comes with enthusiasm. Children are curi-
ous about their environment and are eager to learn. You
can help parents take advantage of this eagerness. Children can be encouraged to learn and can attain an attitude
of joy in learning. Such a basic attitude will be valuable to
them during the years ahead when they might encounter a
boring classroom situation. The joy of learning is a foundation for a lifetime of learning. Mature Christian hope
requires continuous learning and a questing mind in
search of God's mysteries.

Adults can just stand aside and let children learn randomly. Or adults can structure the environment in order to encourage learning. However, educators can go even further. They can systematically encourage some specific attitudes which foster effective learning. Purposiveness and persistence will enhance learning. The appreciation of one's creativity in learning will add to the joy of learning. You can readily deal with these attitudes in the preschool years.

Purposiveness, persistence, and creativity have developmental levels. Each builds step by step. You will find each of the three in the five levels described below.

1. *Newborn.* The roots of purposiveness, persistence, and creativity are all there, but they are very difficult to recognize. Newborns can move approximately one inch by pushing their feet against a barrier. Is that purposiveness? Whatever label you care to use, there is certainly nothing conscious about it on the part of the babies. However, the potential is there.

2. *Infancy.* Watch infants inspect their hands and feet or study a mobile or mouth a toy. Attention becomes very focused. The attention may not last very long, but while it does, it is intense. Creativity as we know it is only a potential. Creativity involves the ability to recognize alternatives, and this ability is beyond the infant's capability.

3. *Toddler.* The discrimination between self and non-self is made. The world spreads out as a huge stage for exploration. There is so much to learn. Toddlers are almost overwhelmed by all the possibilities. Behavior is anything but purposive or persistent. Activity appears to be random, hit or miss, a darting here and there with little rhyme or rea-

son. Children are not yet creative. The nearest thing to creativity that is observed at this level is not creative; it is imitative. Toddlers copy adult behavior, but without imagination. Activity is learning, and a great deal of learning is taking place in a haphazard fashion.

4. *Runabout.* Now you can observe purposiveness and persistence. Children's purpose is to please their parents, but gradually they learn to be purposive and to persist because accomplishment is its own reward. There is pride in completing a simple task. At first, the constant presence of a parent is required. Then, purposiveness and persistence are achieved independently. Creative potential is released with the new capacity of symbolism. Imagination involves the recognition that one object (a block) can be a symbol for something else (a train). The world of makebelieve and fantasy abounds. Fantasy and reality are not clearly distinguishable. The fantasy world of children is real to them. Now is the time to nurture creativity, not to squelch it.[4] Learning is great good fun.

5. *On Beyond.* There are glimpses of a future orientation to purposiveness and persistence. Children constantly practice skills as though they were preparing themselves for what comes next. Even complex tasks can be completed and these children stay with the task until it is completed. Make-believe play gives way to reality play. The doll house kitchen must have all the details in miniature that are found in the family kitchen. The distinction between fantasy and reality is made. Learning is in earnest—there is purpose and persistence. However, parents need to promote imagination and creativity. That is what makes learning a joy.

Jeffrey's father assesses Jeffrey at the Infancy level. He observes Jeffrey carefully as he considers what small step toward level 3 he can make which will contribute to his enjoyment of learning. Jeffrey does not seem to like being cooped up in his playpen. When left there too long he protests loudly. This unique little guy wants to be allowed to roam on all fours. Jeffrey's father's goal:

> "In order to encourage Jeff's learning about the world of the living room, I will baby-proof the room and let him loose to explore under my supervision each day when I get home from work. I will congratulate him when he discovers the couch, the table, the edge of the rug, or whatever he is exploring."

This is another illustration of assessment, step-by-step progression, and goal setting. The uniqueness of Jeffrey has been considered. A plan for reinforcement has been included. And Jeffrey's father is engaged in researching his small explorer.

Two more principles of effective attitude education remain: build on strengths and provide a stimulus. These two principles will be dealt with in the next chapter on love.

Chapter 6

Love

"You shall love the Lord your God with all your heart, and with all your soul, and with all your mind, and with all your strength. . . . You shall love your neighbor as yourself." (Mark 12:29–31 RSV)

Loving God and loving one's neighbor are required of Christians. One cannot meet these claims without faith and hope. Faith, hope, and love, and the greatest of these is love. How can adults fully meet the high standards set forth in the gospel message? You and I are still trying to answer that question and will be seeking the answer for the rest of our lives. Nevertheless, there is one very fundamental aspect of love about which I feel confident. Before I can love as a Christian, I must learn to love myself. I cannot begin to feel loving toward God or others until I have come to terms positively with myself. I came into this world "locked in egocentricity." There was only my self. I will go out of this world the same way, except for love. That is what our faith and hope can bring to us. But it all starts with self.

You must start with self because there is no other place. You are at the headwaters again, trying to decode those precious infants. Newborns have no idea that there is anything other than self, no world out there, no other people, nothing except self. That is scary. The natural reaction of parents is to surround babies with love. They cuddle, fondle, feed, and change diapers. These behaviors are concrete examples of God's love for mankind. Parents are passing on God's love to helpless infants. That is good religious education.

And you can do better. You can help parents to organize their love for their little children by consciously planning to teach two foundational attitudes to their children during the first five years of life. Children can learn:

1. Positive self-regard;
2. Positive orientation to others.

Positive self-regard is a prerequisite for a positive orientation to others. There is a chain reaction here. Love of self—Love of others—Love of God. Of course, the ends of the chain are connected by the link of God's love for each individual.

I will describe the maturity levels once again. In the description of each level, you will see the two-pronged focus of positive self-regard and positive orientation to others.

1. *Newborn.* Newborn babies are unable to make any distinction between self and others. Everything, objects and other people, are merely extensions of self. Out of sight, out of mind describes the newborns' outlook. Something is real only if it can be seen. When an object is removed or a person leaves the room, that object or person no longer exists.

2. *Infancy.* Object constancy has been achieved. When a toy is hidden, children now recognize that the toy still exists. Perceptions sharpen. Parents are recognized, as well as other familiar people. The maturing of perceptions may

result in the babies' fear of strangers. These fears are normal and gradually will be overcome.

3. *Toddler.* The distinction between self and others is made more readily. Periods of shyness with strangers are still normal, but they are diminishing. Toddlers are learning "me," "mine," "you," "yours." True sharing is not yet possible because the concept of possessions is very new. Although toddlers want to please their parents, pleasure is confined to self-pleasure. Many toddlers are very assertive about themselves. They are exploring their independence. Negativism may occur as they test what they can get away with. Other babies are objects to be poked at or shoved. Play with other little children is "parallel play." Children are aware of each other but they are still too immature to risk playing with one another.

4. *Runabout.* Children have again made real progress. If all has gone well up until now, these children are a joy. They feel good about themselves. In their limited world, they have achieved a level of self-confidence. They are beginning to achieve some control over their emotions (but do not expect perfection). Generally, they are positive. They can now accept coaching and advice from adults and, in a very limited sense, they will respond to reason. How do they feel now about others? Cooperative play is beginning. However, when you pay attention to children's conversations, you will notice that the preponderance of talk, either solitary or with another, is essentially self-talk. Also, these children do not yet attribute feelings to others. How they feel is all important. If they feel angry, everyone feels angry. If they feel sad, everyone is sad. Yes, a playmate is recognized as separate from self, but that playmate feels as

I do because I feel that way. I share, I take turns, but the reason I adjust to norms is solely involved in my self-pleasure. However, I am learning social skills because I want to get along with others; that brings me pleasure.

5. *On Beyond.* Again, this is a period of charm that is possible and important to attain before entering school years with new, confusing experiences. These children are positive, cheerful, and self-confident. They not only accept adult guidance, they actively seek such help because they want to improve themselves. As to their relationship to others, they are now able to do two things: (1) they respect adult authority, and (2) they can play cooperatively with peers. There is also further progress. They can now recognize that others have feelings which differ from their own. They can sympathize with other people and they will display sympathy particularly for the underdog. But this is still not empathy. You are still at the headwaters. Children cannot truly roleplay in the sense that they can appreciate another's scope of feelings. But they are on the way. They feel good about themselves and others.

This is the last scale in the faith, hope, and love series. Now I will focus on the last two principles of effective attitude education: (1) building on strengths, and (2) providing a stimulus.

It is appropriate to address the first principle, building on strengths, in relation to love. Building on strengths is a positive approach and love is certainly positive. Listen to Paul's description of love:

"Love is patient; love is kind and envies no one. Love is never boastful, nor conceited, nor rude; never selfish, not quick to take offense. Love keeps no score of wrongs; does

not gloat over other men's sins, but delights in the truth."
(1 Corinthians 13:4–7 New English Bible)

God's love is like this. God helps people to build their
own strengths. God's love "keeps no score of wrongs; does
not gloat over . . . sins, but delights in the truth." Parents
can be like this as they translate God's love to their children. Parents can be quick to forget their children's mis-
takes and errors. How patient and selfless they can be
when it comes to their own children. They delight in their
children's successes. Their concern is for their children's
steps, rather than their stumbles.

Christian attitude education borrows from this model of
good parents. The concept of "building on strengths" adds
power to religious education and renders it far more effective. In fact, one might ask, would education be Christian
without the principle of building on strengths?

Help parents to ask, "What's right about my child? What
are my child's strengths?" Then help them to recognize
that a strength is the place to begin building.

Observe Christy's mother again as she lovingly decides
how to help Christy. First she reads through the maturity
levels of love. She is trying to assess her unique child, and
she is considering Christy's strengths. As an infant, Christy
seemed to be an outgoing little girl. She has readily re-
turned people's smiles ever since she was about six weeks
old. She laughs and reaches out to others. She does not
appreciate being left alone, as she loves being with people.
However, recently her mother has noticed some ap-
prehension on Christy's part when strangers come to the
door. Christy's mother's goal:

"I understand that Chris is getting old enough to recognize all the differences among people. I guess it must be

a little scary for her to confront strange adults. I want to help her move to the Toddler level. I know she has the potential to be outgoing. Tomorrow, my old high school friend is coming to visit. I will observe Chris for any signs of fright. If she is frightened, I will ask my friend to accept Chris's fears, focus the attention level away from Chris and gradually let Chris make the advances. When Chris makes any advances, we will give her just enough attention to make her feel welcome. It may only be that she will come closer or put her hand on my friend's knee. Finally, if Chris wants to be picked up, we will both rejoice in order to reinforce Chris's outgoingness."

That is a long description of a goal. I have expanded the description to illustrate once again all of the principles for attitude education which have been introduced. Christy's mother *assessed* the maturity level of her *unique* child. She is planning a *goal* which is specific as to time and place and her ability to evaluate the results.

In this sense, she is a *researcher* of Christy. She has, in effect, set up an hypothesis: "If I can arrange the environment to match Christy's new perceptual abilities (e.g., explain to my friend that Christy is going through a shy stage), then Christy will gradually assert outgoing behavior in a secure environment." This mother is ready to build with Christy one step in a *step-by-step* process. She has plans for *reinforcing* the behavior that she predicts from Christy. Christy has strengths; uniquely, she is an outgoing little girl. Her mother is lovingly *building on strengths.* She predicts that reinforcement of a past strength, in a loving environment, will sustain Christy's confidence to move forward. To my way of thinking, that is love, God's love, translated by a parent to a child, intentionally, consciously, and within the structure of education. That is what effective religious education is all about at the headwaters of religious education.

One more challenge remains. Although I have touched on the last principle, providing a stimulus, in the illustrations of goal setting, I have yet to deal with it explicitly. This is interesting because in religious education providing a stimulus is traditionally where one *begins*. And yet, stimulus is the last principle which I address. There is a reason for this.

The "why" questions about an educational program are very important. Teachers get hung up on the "how" questions. "How" questions are answered for the educator by the lesson materials or by the curriculum. "Why" questions are addressed by theory and by principles. Do not lose sight of the distinctions between the "hows" and the "whys". Remember the message of the gospel and *why* you are a Christian educator. Somehow or other, in religious education you must weld together theory and practice, the "why" questions and the "how" questions.

Theory is important because it explains, predicts, and verifies reality. I have purposively left the stimulus or lesson materials until last because I wanted first to emphasize the importance of theory. The next chapter will focus on the "hows," the stimuli. However, do not forget that the "why" in attitude education is extremely important.

Fortunately, at the headwaters of religious education when you deal with preschool children, the problem is relatively easy. You can figure out the "why." You are engaged in attitude education because that is the only choice you have. Children are prereligious or preoperational; their senses, their emotions, and their behavior are all you can deal with. Yet what a wonderful opportunity. Religious educators can relate to young children in the affective domain and in the psychomotor domain with the knowledge that growth is also occurring covertly in the cognitive domain. Attitude education for preschool children does not overtly include cognitive goals for intellectual skills. The "whys" of religious attitude education at the preoperational level delineate how to proceed.

Now to close this chapter with an illustration of a helpful stimulus in preschool religious education. The following chapter will deal with stimuli (and reinforcers) in more detail. This last illustration will prepare you for chapter 7.

One last illustration about Jeffrey. The principles I have sketched before will be found, and I will point them out to you. You will recall that the principles are: reinforcement, uniqueness, research, assessment, step-by-step progress, goal setting, building on strengths, in addition to providing a stimulus. However, I am now focusing particularly on providing a *stimulus* which you may understand as the lesson material.

Jeffrey's father has assessed Jeffrey on this chapter's scale at level 3, Toddler. He is interested in helping his son move toward level 4. He decides to concentrate for now on Jeffrey's self-regard. Jeffrey is at the "me mean it," "I do it myself" stage. Jeffrey is testing his independence with a good bit of negativism. He is not very easy to deal with, but his father looks at level 4 and feels hope. He wants to identify that small step of progress that is realistically possible. And he wants to do it with love; he wants to build on strengths.

What will be the stimulus? Here is a story. The lesson material in this case, then, is the story the parent tells to Jeffrey. Jeffrey's parent wants to research his son in order to make an educational plan that fits his unique child. This parent researcher goes to work on his mission as a religious educator and tries, humanely, to do a responsible job. Researching, assessment, step-by-step progress, and recognition of uniqueness receive attention before goal setting occurs. These principles help the parent to understand the "whys" associated with the stimulus. The loving atmosphere of building on strengths answers another "why" of religious education.

Story for Jeffrey The Stimulus	*Remarks*
Once there was a little boy with blue eyes and brown hair.	Jeffrey has blue eyes and brown hair.
He looked just like the little boy in this picture.	Jeffrey is pleased to see a snapshot of himself.
He lived with a mommy, a daddy, and a dog named Spot.	Of course, that is Jeffrey's concrete environment.
He wanted to surprise his father.	Suprises delight little children.
He decided he would help his father pick up all the toys before bedtime.	Nothing is said about all the times Jeffrey has said, "No, I won't."
It was fun and it made his father very happy. Mommy noticed the little boy being such a big help. She was pleased and gave her little boy a piggyback ride to bed.	The anticipated reinforcement makes Jeffrey feel good.

   Jeffrey's goal: "At bedtime, I will tell Jeffrey a story about a little boy who makes his father happy by helping him pick up toys. If Jeffrey helps me pick up the toys tomorrow, I will thank him and give him a hug."

You may not like Jeffrey's story.[1] True, it is no literary masterpiece. On the other hand, it "fits" Jeffrey. It is a stimulus for him to try a new behavior. It is at his level of development and matches his own uniqueness. Will the stimulus result in Jeffrey's helping with the toys the next day? Maybe and maybe not. If the story does not work, there are many other stories about children feeling good as a result of helping their parents. There are animal stories as well. Perhaps Jeffrey's mother would be a more effective storyteller. Perhaps the stimulus at a different time of day would work better. All of these approaches are cumulative and chances are that one day Jeffrey will decide, "Yes, I will help pick up the toys." That is the time to reinforce the learner. Every time Jeffrey repeats the helping behavior, he should be reinforced until he is a helper by habit. A helper is on the way to becoming a loving Christian with positive self-regard.

Chapter 7

Nuts and Bolts—Reinforcers and Stimuli

Nuts and bolts go together. Thus, this chapter will deal with both reinforcers and stimuli. The reinforcer is the "nut" of the matter which "bolts" down the stimuli. I will begin this chapter with some theory (learning theory) but I will soon move to an applied level and then conclude with very specific illustrations in the religious education of preschool children.

I have skirted around learning theory[1] with terms like "stimuli" and "reinforcers." Now it is time to be more direct. However, I do not propose to give you a course in the multiplicity of learning theories. I do propose to describe theories which will be helpful as you consider reinforcers and stimuli.

In classical conditioning, a stimulus and a response are associated (learned) by the learner. In simplest terms, the teacher can replace an unconditioned stimulus with a conditioned stimulus in order to evoke the response. This is not very satisfactory to the educator whose goal is not to change stimuli but to change responses. The teacher knows that learning has occurred when the learner gives evidence of a changed behavior in response to a lesson. However, retain the idea of stimuli evoking a response for the time being.

A stimulus and a response are also associated in operant conditioning. Yet the emphasis is on the response side of the S-R paradigm. The teacher waits until the learner responds in a desired manner and then strengthens the association by reinforcing the learner for the response. Remarkable feats of learning can be achieved not only with Skinner's pigeons but also with human learners. Programmed instruction is based on operant conditioning. The learner is rewarded when responses are desired but not when the response is not desired. Behavior therapy is based on operant conditioning in the same way. Yet there is more than meets the eye here. Teachers who use operant conditioning do not ignore the stimulus. For example, Skinner put his pigeons in cages where there was not much else to do other than peck at buttons. He manipulated the environment in order to provide opportunity for the S-R interaction in which he was interested. Certainly, a learner engaged in programmed instruction with a machine has had the environment arranged. Behavior therapy is yet another example of manipulating the environment in order optimally to achieve desired responses which then can be reinforced.

"Manipulating the environment" sounds like rearranging the furniture. Better terms might be "to stimulate" or "to challenge" the learner. This is still operant conditioning because teachers must still wait for the learners to respond in a desired manner so that the response can be reinforced. However, by paying attention to a stimulus as a stimulator or challenge, you enhance your chances of success.

Reinforce desired behavior; do not reinforce undesired behavior. Through this selective reaction to various behaviors, teachers can strengthen desired behavior and extinguish undesired behavior. One final word of help from learning psychologists: reinforce desired behavior after every response until the behavior is firmly established. Thereafter, intermittent reinforcements will be sufficient to maintain the behavior.

I have purposefully reduced learning theory to very simple components not because theory is simple or because you do not need to know more about it. My purpose has been to give you explanations that can readily be understood and used by parents. Of course, some parents are already acquainted with learning theory and others who are not will want more exposure. That is a special problem where your expertise will be called upon. What you have found here is only a beginning which is particularly important in the attitude education of very young children by their parents.

STIMULI—THE BOLTS

I have indicated previously that the stimulus, or challenge to the learner, is the curriculum or lesson. Of course, with preschool children and particularly with babies, the learner is not "taught" a lesson in any traditional sense. The learner is challenged to try a new behavior which can be reinforced. That which challenges babies will not challenge nursery school children and vice versa. Also, children are unique and children at the same developmental level will respond uniquely. This is one reason parents must research their children.

However, stimuli can be categorized. The number of applicable categories expands with developmental level.

Thus, stimuli will be organized by the familiar levels of Newborn, Infancy, Toddler, Runabout, and On Beyond. The categories will be: Sensory, Motor, Preoperational Cognitive, and Intrinsic. These categories relate to the type of response the stimuli elicit.

SENSORY STIMULI

The five senses are, of course, to see, to hear, to smell, to taste, and to touch. The use of any of the senses or, more exactly, the opportunity to use any of the senses is stimulating to the child. Newborns are challenged by parents' touch or voice, by the feeling of a full tummy and dry, clean clothes. Infants are challenged by mobiles, toys for grasping, noises to be made by banging, etc. However, at these early developmental levels before object constancy is attained, children have no sense of "This is an X (a stimulus) that results in a Y (a reinforcer)." Cause and effect are unknown to babies, but they need not be to parents. Babies learn by continually experiencing. Feeding is reinforced by cuddling. Babies' smiles in response to the parents' smiles are reinforced by parents' behaviors of delight. The mobile elicits kicking and reaching. This kicking and reaching activity is reinforced by sounds of approval from parents. Feeding, parents' smiles, and the mobile are sensory stimulators which can be paired with a reinforcer. Each response must be reinforced for babies and, more importantly, it is best not to confuse babies with inconsistent reinforcement. Parents should not scowl at smiling babies or ignore their kicking and reaching activities.

Sensory stimuli increase in number for toddlers although many of these stimuli can be used in the last half of the first year. Here is a list of some sensory stimuli to challenge toddlers to learn.[2]

Simple Stories	Musical Instruments
Pictures	Jingles
Flash Cards	New Foods
Posters	Different Textured Objects
Art Materials	Different Tasting Foods

You can probably think of other stimuli. All during the preschool years sensory stimuli will challenge young learners. However, the challenges become more sophisticated with increasing maturity.

MOTOR STIMULI

The first list of stimuli was a list of sensory stimuli. A list of motor stimuli might look like this:

Mobiles	Rocking horse	Tricycles/bicycles
Blocks	Push/Pull toys	Construction sets
Stuffed animals	Nesting utensils	Swimming pools
Rattles	Pots and pans	Athletic equipment
Balls	Puzzles	Family games
Walker	Playground equipment	Play-acting props

Newborn
Infant | Toddler | ← Runabout ⟶ On Beyond

I have grouped motor stimuli by developmental level as indicated by the levels beneath the lists. However, as indicated by the arrows, there is a good bit of overlap. Some infants love pots and pans, some toddlers are great at swimming and some runabouts still enjoy a rockinghorse.

The list, of course, is incomplete. Motor stimuli are those things which stimulate motor activity.

PREOPERATIONAL COGNITIVE STIMULI

This category of stimuli becomes important to the teacher attempting to challenge children during the cognitive shift from the sensory-motor stage to the preoperational stage. The shift begins with object constancy at the end of infancy but is not completed until many months later. However, cognitive stimuli are useful even before the preoperational stage is fully attained. That is, the stimuli are useful if, in fact, they do challenge children to think.

Hide & seek games	Tools	Science kits
Form boards	Puzzles	Explanations
Stacking games	Sorting games	Construction sets
Flash cards	Doll house	Reading-readiness games

Again, I have ordered these suggestions by developmental level starting in late infancy. Again, there is overlap between levels and, again, the list is not intended to be complete. However, now you are aware of another overlap. I have purposely repeated some stimulators that you found in previous lists. For example, construction sets were found under Motor Stimuli. The categories of stimuli overlap. This is natural because children engage in motor activities which demand the use of the senses and the use of cognition.

INTRINSIC STIMULI[3]

Have you ever observed an older preschooler who has just completed a picture, built a castle, or set the table perfectly? Have you seen a comical look of smug satisfaction? Pleasure in achievement stimulates more picture painting, more castles, and more table setting. In fact, as children discover success in a few activities, they are apt to be self-motivated to try new activities. They build a set of self stimuli which hopefully will work a lifetime for them.

A full cycle has been completed with the S-R paradigm. An original stimulus has evoked a response which now becomes a stimulus for a next response. For example, the construction set was the original stimulus. Kim responded to the stimulus by building a castle. The finished product was a beautiful construction. Kim's success reinforced him. The success stimulated (was a stimulus for) him to respond by next building a ship with his construction set. At the same time, Kim is learning the attitudes for purposefulness, persistence, and positive self-regard. When teachers can use stimuli in order to successfully stimulate self-motivation in the learners, then education itself has been a success. However, it cannot be done without reinforcers, the "nuts" that "bolt" together the S-R interaction.

REINFORCERS—THE NUTS

Reinforcers can be "nuts" for the "bolts" only if they cause children to feel good about self. At the beginnings of religious education, it is as simple as that. A successful reinforcer gives the learners pleasure. If the children do not feel pleasure, reinforcement has not occurred. Of course, that which gives runabouts pleasure differs from that which gives infants pleasure. And again, children at a similar developmental level are still unique and need to be researched as to what gives each pleasure. The categories of reinforcers will be inspected; at the same time, attention will be paid to levels. The categories will be: Physical, Verbal, Concrete, and Intrinsic. The derivation of these categories is related to development, as I shall explain.

PHYSICAL REINFORCERS

Physical reinforcers are important for all preschool children but particularly for newborns and infants. There are no other reinforcers available during the earliest months, the sensorimotor period. Anything which a child perceives through the five senses and which brings pleasure is a physical reinforcer. Parents cuddle babies and the babies are reinforced by the signs of love and security. Actually, babies are made to feel good about self. Before babies go much beyond the first half year, a distinction between physical contact and other physical signs of comfort and approval needs to be made. Parents' smiles or even just approving nods are physical reinforcers. Some toddlers, particularly at the negativistic stage when they are striving for independence, find hugs and kisses demeaning. They do need smiles or nods, though, to reinforce approved behavior.

Some children may resist physical contact at one time and be made to feel good by physical contact at another time. When independent toddlers receive a severe scare, often it is only physical contact with parents that can reinforce.

There is another aspect to physical reinforcers which needs attention. What is it about reinforcers that makes them reinforcers? I have said before that reinforcers make children feel good, they give pleasure. How do they give pleasure? Newborns are reinforced by physical comfort. As egocentricity diminishes and babies make the distinction between self and others, parental attention and approval give pleasure. Little children wish to please their parents because if they receive parental approval, life will tend to be pleasant. When parental approval is lacking, the situation is not nearly so pleasant for the child. Hugs or pats are signs of approval. Smiles and nods are signs of approval.

VERBAL REINFORCERS

The spoken word can be a reinforcer as soon as children attain understanding of words. Most one-year-old babies understand "good boy," "good girl," "that's good," and "yes" long before they can speak the words. As toddlers master the spoken language, the power of verbal reinforcers increases. The runabout is reinforced for coping behaviors by simple explanations and information. They are reinforced in their attempt to learn skills by parents' coaching and guidance through the spoken word.

Parents' approval is easily conveyed by words of praise. When parents carefully listen as children speak words, this attention is a powerful reinforcer. Listening is an important reinforcer if it is used correctly. Jennifer has drawn a picture and is explaining the meaning of the parts of her picture to her father. Her father listens attentively. He may even ask a few questions. Jennifer is reinforced. The parent has used listening correctly. All too often parents listen just long enough to collect items to be criticized and corrected. That kind of feedback to children is not reinforcing. It is very discouraging to toddlers and runabouts whose creations (pictures, make-believe houses, buildings, towers, etc.) are real to them. Parents should not criticize when their intention is to reinforce.

CONCRETE REINFORCERS

Physical reinforcers and verbal reinforcers are parental behaviors. Concrete reinforcers are rewards which are given to children. They are usually objects, but they could include going for a ride, visiting the playground, or having a friend visit. Those special occasions are a sub-category. I will focus attention on object rewards for the time being with the realization that much of what you will read applies to special occasions, particularly if the question of bribing a child is on your mind.

Parents may have reservations about the use of concrete rewards. "I don't want my child to expect prizes for every good behavior." The difficulty here is partly a matter of false assumptions, if you assume that rewards are habit-forming. Another difficulty is the failure to realize that little children are self-pleasure seekers and frequently take rewards during the course of each day. A sucked thumb is a reward. A security blanket is a reward. A favorite stuffed animal is a reward. When you use concrete rewards as reinforcers, you are consciously using a technique which is natural and normal for the small pleasure seekers.

Rewards can be as simple as a gold star on the refrigerator door, a handful of raisins, a picture card, a poster, a piece of apple, a walk in the park, or a ride in the car. The reward can be accompanied by, "I like what you just did. We will put a star on the refrigerator." Children may not understand all of the words, but they do understand the star that shines clear and bold for everyone to see.

A concrete reward is a way of communicating parental approval. At the infancy and toddler stages, concrete rewards are motivators. They are effective in moving children on to a more mature level of motivation. Parental approval is extremely important as a motivator to encourage dependent toddlers toward greater independence. With independence comes a new motivator—pleasure in achievement. This is an inner motivation. But educators build toward this goal by providing external reinforcers, or concrete rewards.

INTRINSIC REINFORCERS

Intrinsic reinforcement occurs when little children can reinforce themselves by their own pride in their accomplishments. Educators who have helped them along the way can feel pride, too. Learners have matured beyond the point of desiring adult approval, although this reinforcer will still be important. In order to cement intrinsic reinforcers in the S-R paradigm, attention should be given to all reinforcers. Parents can use a number of reinforcers simultaneously. Intrinsic reinforcers are not suddenly available on Thursday evening at 7:00 p.m. Self-motivation builds gradually. Parents can reinforce self-motivation.

There are a number of ways to reinforce self-motivation. Physical, verbal, and concrete reinforcers can be used in order to bolster children's satisfaction with their accomplishments. Give Eddie a hug, some words of praise, or a star on his chart when he gets every piece into the puzzle board. Listen to Jennifer as she explains her finger painting and say, "I like your picture." Another way to reinforce pride in accomplishment is to put the production on display for all to see. These more mature preschoolers are charmed by as extensive an audience as is available. The only warning I would give is not to overdo it. Self-satisfaction should be reinforced. Arrogance should not be reinforced. Help your parents to reinforce pride in achievement only up to the point where it is firmly incorporated as an intrinsic reinforcer.

STIMULUS-REINFORCEMENT INTERACTION

Stimuli and reinforcers have been treated separately thus far. They do, of course, belong together. Just as a stimulus and a response are "associated" when learning takes place, so must stimuli and reinforcers be bonded in the teaching process. One without the other is not effective teaching. Together, nuts and bolts are effective. However, the effectiveness is strengthened by the other principles of attitude education: uniqueness, researching, assessment, step-by-step progress, goal setting, and building on strengths. All of the principles are necessary for effective attitude education.

In religious education particularly, there is one more ingredient. I am speaking now about the parents' attitudes. The background music for the stimulus-reinforcement interaction must be parents' love, understanding, and patience.

There is more that can be said about stimuli and reinforcers. My lists were not complete. There is more that can be said about the stimuli-reinforcer interaction. I will close this chapter will illustrations of religious education in action. Often illustrations can accomplish more than paragraphs of prose. These illustrations come from real-life protocols[4] from parents. They are organized for you by the familiar developmental levels of Newborn, Infancy, Toddler, Runabout, and On Beyond.

The illustrations are also organized by my categories of faith, hope, and love. Faith, hope, and love, after all, are the ultimate goals of religious education. While I have gone into learning theory, stimuli, and reinforcers, the ultimate goals have been set aside. It is appropriate now to bring faith, hope, and love back into focus as the eight principles and the stimulus-reinforcement interaction in parents' religious education of their preschool children are illustrated. In the following illustrations, Educational Goals refers to the progress possible during the preschool years toward the ultimate goals of mature faith, hope, and love. Thus, as you read the illustrations you will be reviewing those educational goals. Procedures are strategies parents plan to use in order to make progress just one step at a time.

Illustrations

NEWBORN

FAITH

  Educational Goal

    The child can learn to trust the dependability of the parent.

  Procedure

    "When Lisa cries, I will go to her and try to comfort her."

Educational Goal
The child can learn to appreciate nature.
Procedure
"When Greg is distressed, I will check clothing for warmth and dryness and will rock him."
Educational Goal
The child can have faith in the predictability of events.
Procedure
"When Lynn wakes and frets, I will try nursing her."

HOPE

Educational Goal
The child can attain a positive attitude toward life.
Procedure
"I will purchase a rocking chair and rock Eddie."
Educational Goal
The child can learn to be joyful about learning.
Procedure
"I will put a colorful poster on the inner side of Tim's crib."

LOVE

Educational Goal
The child can begin to have a positive self-regard.
Procedure
"I will place Karen #1 in my priorities."
Educational Goal
The child can begin to have a positive orientation to others.
Procedure
"Whenever I am with Kim, I will talk or sing in order to make verbal contact."

INFANCY

FAITH

Educational Goal

The child can learn to trust the dependability of the parent.

Procedure

"My goal is to help Cathy to trust me. The stimulus is milk. The reinforcement is cradling in my arms during nursing or bottle feeding."

Educational Goal

The child can learn to appreciate nature.

Procedure

"I want Greg to enjoy the out-of-doors. We will go out whenever the weather is good (stimulus), and I will encourage any signs of Greg's delight by signs of my pleasure (reinforcer)."[5]

Educational Goal

The child can have faith in the predictability of events.

Procedure

"Lynn's bathtime will be at the same time every day (stimulus), and we will enjoy it by laughing together (reinforcer)."

HOPE

Educational Goal

The child can attain a positive attitude toward life.

Procedure

"First, I will get Kim to smile and gurgle by making funny faces (stimulus); then I will laugh and smile, too (reinforcer)."

Educational Goal

The child can learn to be joyful about learning.

Procedure

"My goal is to help Chris enjoy learning. The stimulus is an interesting toy placed just beyond her reach. The reinforcement is my exclamations of delight as she wiggles over to grasp the toy."

LOVE

Educational Goal

The child can begin to have positive self-regard.

Procedure

"I will help Mike feel positive about himself. The stimulus is the opportunity for Mike to try out a new walker. The reinforcement is my praise when Mike accepts the challenge and moves about in the walker."

Educational Goal

The child can begin to have a positive orientation to others.

Procedure

"I will play peek-a-boo with Eddie (stimulus). When he enjoys our game, I will laugh and hug him (reinforcer)."

TODDLER

FAITH

Educational Goal

The child can learn to trust the dependability of the parent.

Procedure

"Lisa is striving for independence. In fact, she does not even want me in the same room when she starts her supper. However, by the end of the meal when she gets tired, she wants my help. I will respect her independence and go elsewhere as she begins to eat, but I will be on hand when the whimpering begins (stimulus). I will help her finish eating (reinforcer)."

Educational Goal

The child can learn to appreciate nature.

Procedure

"We will watch the sunset tonight. The stimulus will be my behaviors which express enthusiasm and awe. If Jeff imitates my behaviors, I will reinforce him by putting my arm around him while we view the beauty together."

Educational Goal

The child can have faith in the predictability of events.

Procedure.

"I will provide the stimulus of a toy that can be pulled at will. Jennifer can walk well now, and she loves to pull toys. The goal is to get her to trust the cause and effect sequence. If I give her the pull toy, I predict that she will figure out how to pull it. If in fact she does, I will reinforce Jennifer with a hug to show her that I approve."

HOPE

Educational Goal

The child can attain a positive attitude toward life.

Procedure

"Christy can learn to laugh at minor bumps and scratches. I will draw a picture of a smiling clown and put it on the refrigerator as a stimulus. I will tell Christy that the clown is smiling even though he just bumped into a chair. When Christy bumps into something I will blow away the hurt and see if she will laugh and smile. If she does, I will paste a star on the clown picture for her (reinforcer)."

Educational Goal

The child can learn to be joyful about learning.

Procedure

"The goal is for Sean to enjoy exploring and learning in the bathtub. At bathtime tonight I will take two plastic cups and show Sean a new game of pouring water from one cup to the other (stimulus). If Sean enjoys this, we will laugh and play together in order to reinforce his joy in learning something new."

RUNABOUT

FAITH

Educational Goal

The child can learn to trust the dependability of the parent.

Procedure

"Karen will accept guidance and coaching now. In fact, she is after me all the time about learning how to ride her bicycle. She can depend on me. I will spend a half hour each day helping her learn (stimulus) and I will praise every step toward her success (reinforcer)."

Educational Goal

The child can learn to appreciate nature.

Procedure

"Karen's goal is to learn more about nature by having a little garden of her own. As I do the tasks in the big garden (stimulus) Karen can imitate me in her little garden. This will go on all summer so I will have to praise her constantly (reinforcer) for being such a good worker. I can explain about seeds growing into plants (stimulus). When her flowers begin to blossom she will be proud of what she has accomplished (reinforcer)."

Educational Goal

The child can have faith in the predictability of events.

Procedure

"Tim is anxious to be prepared for what comes next. He wants to play in the games of the older children, but he cannot run fast enough yet. If he can improve his running skills, the other children will accept him. I will tell him the story of the Wise Owl who told the little squirrel to practice and practice running (stimulus). Whenever I see Tim practicing running, I will praise him (reinforcer)."

HOPE

Educational Goal

The child can attain a positive attitude toward life.

Procedure

"Christy's imagination is full-blown. Her present craze is with space ships to the moon. I can have fun telling her science fiction stories (stimulus), and I can go on a make-believe space ride with her (stimulus). I will show her by my behavior that I am having fun (reinforcer)."

Educational Goal

The child can learn to be joyful about learning.

Procedure

"Eddie's goal is to work toward the attitude of joy in learning. In order to get Eddie to enjoy careful and thorough work as he attempts to learn to build with his construction set, I will tell him a story (stimulus) about a boy who had an elf on each shoulder; one was named Checkers and the other was named Slipshod. Each advised the boy on how to build a tall tower. Whose advice did the boy take? If Eddie builds his tower very carefully, I will put it on display for all to see (reinforcer). I will put a Checkers the Elf picture on Eddie's chart (reinforcer).

LOVE

Educational Goal

The child can learn to have positive self-regard.

Procedure

"Amy's goal is to gain confidence in her art work. I will give her the paper, brushes, and poster paint and ask her to draw a picture of our family (stimulus). When her painting has been completed, I will listen while she tells me about it (reinforcer). I will not criticize or tell her how I think it should be done, but I will show my interest in her painting."

Educational Goal

The child can learn a positive orientation toward others.

Procedure

"Jennifer's goal is to feel positive about her friend who is coming to visit. I will show her how to greet her friend, hang up her coat, offer her juice and crackers, and introduce a few games. We will act out (stimulus) these social skills together. She can be herself, and I will pretend to be her friend. Tomorrow after her friend's visit, we will spend a few minutes talking together about her successes and I will praise her for her accomplishments (reinforcer)."

ON BEYOND

FAITH

Educational Goal

The child can learn to trust the dependability of authority figures.

Procedure

"Mike has discovered that his parents do not know everything. He needs to learn that there are other people and sources where he can get help. We will go to the library tomorrow. Mike has questions about thunder and lightning. We will get to know the librarian and find some books about storms. I will reinforce Mike in his seeking for information."

Educational Goal

The child can learn to appreciate nature.

Procedure

"Our cat is about to have kittens. What an opportunity to explain to Lyn God's plan in reproduction. Probably the birth of the kittens will be reinforcement enough, but I will share with Lyn my awe and excitement about the arrival of the kittens."

Educational Goal

The child can have faith in the predictability of events.

Procedure

"Tommy is looking forward to school in the fall. We will get a calendar (stimulus) and mark off the days (reinforcer)."

HOPE

Educational Goal

The child can attain a positive attitude toward life.

Procedure

"We will make a Happy Times chart and put it on Cathy's bedroom door. Day-by-day Cathy can report on her happy times, and I will write it on the chart. Her mother will be delighted, as will I."

Educational Goal

The child can learn to be joyful about learning.

Procedure

"Terry is beginning to understand the difference between real and make-believe. We do not want him to lose the creativity associated with make-believe, but we do want to help with distinctions. I will make a set of flash cards of real people and make-believe people. We will have fun together identifying each card."

LOVE

Educational Goal

The child can learn to have positive self-regard.

Procedure

"Mike is pleased when he completes a task. He and his mother are refinishing the toy chest in the basement. I will tell Mike the story of Grandfather Followthrough and I will make a poster of Grandfather Followthrough with squares to check off as Mike completes each part of the task. Mike will be proud of the completed toy chest and he'll also be delighted as all the squares on the poster are checked off."

Educational Goal

The child can learn positive orientations to others.

Procedure

"Melanie is beginning to recognize that others have feelings not necessarily of the kind she experiences.

We will act out together with hand puppets how Wise Owl tells Jeffrey Squirrel how it hurts his playmate when Jeffrey Squirrel kicks him. His playmate has feelings, too. We will praise Melanie when she resists kicking and when she comforts her little brother."

Chapter 8

Freedom and Dignity—
Intrinsic Conditioning

"Freedom and dignity" is a phrase borrowed, of course, from the title of a book by B. F. Skinner.[1] Essentially Skinner has no use for freedom and dignity. The complete title of his book is *Beyond Freedom and Dignity.* However, I would like to make the point that religious education is education for freedom and dignity.

In the last chapter, categories of stimuli and reinforcers were inspected. The most mature category of both stimuli and reinforcers was intrinsic. Learners self-stimulate and learners self-reinforce. That is freedom and dignity. Learners become self-learners with self-control over the person-environment interaction. The concept of a free and dignified learner is a mature and ideal concept. Therefore, it is well to back up a bit and make the attempt to describe an educational process which is rational and applicable. In the attempt I will review what I have been promoting as attitude education all along. This reminds me of the preaching technique used so effectively by Harry Emerson Fosdick. Start with illustrations of all the pieces of the puzzle and then, at the conclusion solve the puzzle with the text of the sermon.

The text, in this case, is intrinsic conditioning.[2] Here is a review of the pieces of the puzzle. First, you were given eight principles of attitude education: assessment, progression step-by-step, research, uniqueness, goal setting, building on strengths, stimuli, and reinforcement. Next, in order to illustrate their application in religious education, I applied those eight principles to faith, hope, and love. However, the principles of stimuli and reinforcement were focused upon last in order to emphasize the importance of the first six principles. Stimuli and reinforcement are basic to any educational endeavor. I believe they are enhanced in any endeavor in attitude education by the practice of the other six principles. Moreover, I think the other six principles are essential in religious education, particularly at the infancy-preschool level.

I have repeatedly called attention to the parents' understanding, patience, and love in their educational ministry to their preschool children. Religious educators have a certain assurance that these attitudes are present in parents in appreciable amounts, at least during the initial months with their newborn babies. The principles of assessment, progression step-by-step, research, uniqueness, goal setting, and particularly building on strengths operationalize these parental attitudes. Knowledge of these principles can channel parents' initial understanding, patience, and love. Or should I say parents' faith, hope, and love for their children?

The principles of assessment, research, and uniqueness reinforce the parents' understanding. The principles of progression step-by-step and goal setting reinforce the parents' love. Stimuli and reinforcers can be used within the framework of the other principles to tie the endeavors all together into a practical, effective educational adventure for parents.

As I moved another step closer to intrinsic conditioning,

there was further clarification of the stimuli and reinforcers dealt with in the last chapter. I have purposely not emphasized theory or theology because I want this book to be for religious educators who must deal with parents. Also, while my knowledge of learning theory is adequate, my knowledge of theology is unsophisticated at best. However, with the knowledge and experience, both basic and applied, to which I can lay claim, I have thought at great length about these relationships and exactly how they affect attitude education.

I would like to go back to the S-R paradigm. Furthermore, I would like to use the S-R paradigm to illustrate graphically a progression from Newborns' learning to mature On Beyond children's learning. This will lead toward intrinsic conditioning.

$$\text{⑤- R}$$

That is a graphic representation of Pavlovian or classical conditioning. I do not want parents to be obsessed with influencing stimuli. My purpose in drawing Pavlov to your attention was to keep your attention on stimuli, although I will admit that I changed from stimuli as the antecedent of a response to stimuli as the stimulator to optimally elicit a response. Nonetheless, with newborns the distinction between stimuli and reinforcers is vague. The new babies have no schema for dealing with any distinctions. Yet parents must be encouraged to make distinctions as they understand, have patience with, and love budding learners.

During children's infancy, you are given your first clear opportunity to move beyond a possible ⑤ – R toward an S – ⑧.

I put the circle around the R to indicate the Skinnerian

approach. The emphasis is on reinforcing the response. As I have previously pointed out, educational achievements of magnitude have been achieved through operant conditioning. My belief is that operant conditioning is a powerful tool which religious educators should use themselves and teach parents how to use. What other way is there in the beginnings of religious education? Preoperational children cannot rationalize the way adults can. However, loving adults can condition children's behavior in such a way as to pave the way for positive attitudes.

There is no doubt in my mind that for older infants, toddlers, and runabouts the emphasis on S-(R) is essential. This is the rational and only starting point. Normal preschool children want their parents' approval and their own self-pleasure. What better way to elicit behavior than with rewards which give self-pleasure and demonstrate approval.

I hope that I have shown you how to use operant conditioning in such a way that you can pass the knowledge on to parents. Reinforce, reinforce, and reinforce. Yet, the teachers (the parents) should reinforce with understanding, patience, and love. The other tools are assessment, research, uniqueness, progression step-by-step, goal setting, building on strengths, and, finally, stimuli. Again, I repeat that I have superimposed a stimulator-reinforcer paradigm upon the traditional S–R paradigm. However, I do it with reason. I want to demonstrate the potential of the progression from (S)-R (Pavlovian conditioning) to S-(R) (Skinnerian conditioning) to (S)(R) (intrinsic conditioning).

I believe that education at its best is education aimed toward intrinsic conditioning. I further believe that religious education must direct itself toward intrinsic conditioning. There are many religious educators who will think that I am way out in left field. Perhaps I am. Yet is religious education only interested in the infield? My argument is for the necessity of educating players for the entire ball park. The best ball player intrinsically is conditioned to respond to the entire ball park of life.

Intrinsic conditioning is still a hazy ideal. Educate learners to provide their own stimuli and their own reinforcers! It is possible. The noncollege business successes are self-learners. The graduate-school successes are self-learners. And, I would add, committed Christians are self-learners.

Intrinsic conditioning is a possibility in education. The progression from Ⓢ-R to S-Ⓡ and then to Ⓢ Ⓡ is a reality for education. Religious educators must care about the freedom and dignity of learners. Freedom and dignity are ideals, they are ultimate goals. I ask you to return to the ultimate goals of faith, hope, and love and ask yourself if they are possible without the freedom and dignity accessible through intrinsic conditioning. My definition of faith was "trust in a God creator and the self-confidence to accept God's grade." Does operant conditioning accomplish this kind of faith? Trust, perhaps, can be accomplished through operant conditioning. However, accepting God's grace is initiated by the individual. Intrinsic conditioning is called for.

My definition for hope was twofold: "(1) reliance on the kingdom of God now and hereafter, and (2) trust in the potential for obtaining greater knowledge and understanding of the unknown." Again, operant conditioning may accomplish the first, but intrinsic conditioning is necessary for the second. Obtaining greater knowledge and understanding of the unknown requires a self-learner.

Loving God and loving one's neighbor are required of Christians. Such loving is possible only with faith and hope. Therefore, mature love necessitates intrinsic conditioning. Commitment must be self-initiated. The term has no meaning without intrinsic conditioning. Intrinsic conditioning and the faith, hope, and love thus made possible are the ultimate goals of religious education. It is your responsibility to aim toward such lofty goals. Assist your learners toward freedom and dignity in their quest for the unknown.

At the headwaters of religious education, I have tried to show you how to begin, through parents, the attitude education of infants and preschoolers. I identified foundational attitudes for faith, hope, and love which are possible to teach to little children. Moreover, I built toward intrinsic conditioning systematically and consistently.

The methods available to you will not automatically result on the sixth birthday in a self-motivated learner. However, the groundwork will have been laid. The chances for freedom and dignity in tle late teens and adult life will have been greatly enhanced. Parents must continue the process of S-$\textcircled{R}$ to $\textcircled{S}$-$\textcircled{R}$ throughout their children's lives. You must support the process in church school and in youth groups—wherever you encounter the budding Christian. Attitude education toward intrinsic conditioning is religious education. It must continue at all age levels. Religious education never ends. This is a life cycle orientation. I have dealt with only the preschool level, but I would like to conclude with one further insight.

As you teach parents how to teach their preschool children in religious attitudes, do not overlook the parents themselves as learners. You will be influencing the religious education at two periods in the life cycle, the beginnings and young adulthood. As parents learn the principles of attitude education and engage in teaching foundational attitudes for faith, hope, and love to their children, you can be reinforcing their own intrinsic conditioning. Parents will begin to question their own faith, hope, and love. They can begin to use the eight principles with themselves. You will have a golden opportunity not only to influence the little children but also to assist in the continuing religious education of parents.

If I have been successful in my purpose for writing this book, you now have the essentials for planning a program for your parents. You may work in the home with individual couples. You may plan meetings for groups of parents in homes. You may plan meetings for parents in the church. The situation will differ in each parish and you must decide upon your best approach.

However, the need is there. Hopefully, you now have the means with which to meet the need.

When Jesus said, "Let the children come to me . . . ," he was teaching adults. You can put new blood into religious education and go and do likewise.

Chapter 9

The Bible

Now that you know the methodology for attitude education, I will focus on how you can apply that methodology. The application so far has been in terms of parent education in that methodology. Teach parents the educational goals and the eight principles of attitude education. That is an essential first step. However, the parents have not really learned new skills until they have practiced the new skills. They need resources available to them. Think of all the resources available in the secular society: TV, recordings, libraries, zoos, daycare centers, nursery schools, shopping centers, public transportation, . . . the list can go on and on. I will confine myself to the resources available to parents over which you have influence or in which you have a direct interest. This chapter and following chapters will deal with Bible, Prayer, Church as Community, Worship Services, and, finally, Church School.

THE BIBLE AS A RESOURCE

One of the best ways to introduce little children to God and Jesus is through stories. The best resource for stories about God and Jesus is the Bible. Unfortunately, many parents have difficulty recognizing the Bible as a resource for stories, or, if they do recognize the Bible as a resource, they fail to know how to use it. You can help the parents in your parish to recognize that the Bible is a resource. You can also show them how to use it with their little children.

Children love to be read to or told a story. One reason, of course, is that they enjoy the total attention of the adult. They can appreciate the warm, physical contact that usually accompanies a story, particularly if they are cuddled on their parent's lap. From the point of view of attitude education, a story is a stimulus which encourages a new behavior. Thus, stories can be chosen which are related to an educational goal. For example, if the educational goal is helping the children feel good about themselves and if the strategy is to get the children to say, "Jesus loves me," use the story of Jesus calling the little children (Luke 19:15-16. RSV).

Lest you believe that I view the Bible as a resource for stories only, let me point out another use. The language of some of the passages of the Bible thrills all of us. Even children can appreciate the grandeur of the words. They may want to memorize some verses, not that they will understand them in the ways that adults can understand them. Here is an example. The educational objective is appreciation of nature. The goal is to stimulate the children to look at the hills. What better vehicle than the 121st psalm, "I will lift up my eyes to the hills ...." Verses learned by little children may last a lifetime with greater and clearer understanding coming gradually with age and maturity. In attitude education, it is attitudes, beliefs, and values that are nurtured. Intellectual understanding of content is not the aim with preschool children.

Before I inspect developmental levels and more educational goals for faith, hope, and love, consider some broad aspects about the Bible. It is called the Holy Bible. It is sacred and central in Christian life. The Bible is certainly not treated as just any book. There is a special shelf for the Bible in homes. There is a special lectern for the Bible in churches. The Bible is important, and it is treated with respect.

You can help parents to model this respectful behavior toward the Bible for their children. Children are great imitators and they want to please their parents. They soon understand that it will displease their parents should they scribble or tear pages in the Bible. In fact, they can learn to look at a Bible only when a parent is reading a verse to them or is supervising their looking and touching. If this sounds harsh or overly cautious, I would suggest that you tell parents to buy some books of Bible stories with lots of pictures, of course, and give these to the children. The Bible is a resource to the parents. It is a library of stories and treasured verses. Parents go to the Bible to find stories or verses which are appropriate for their children.

I believe that it is beneficial for children to see their parents studying the Bible. For many adults this means writing notes in the margins of the Bible. However, the Bible is an adult book, not a children's book. That is why I suggest a picture book of Bible stories for children to own. If children want to imitate studying behaviors, let them do so with their own books which are related to the Bible. However, in order to encourage respect for holy scripture, parents can retain ownership of the book itself. The Bible belongs to all ages. The book which is a physical object belongs to adults and youth. The book requires advanced reading skills which preschool children do not possess. Yet the Bible as a symbol is a concept children can begin to appreciate if they are taught the attitudes of respect for an object of importance to their parents.

I have suggested picture books of Bible stories for the

children. However, I do not recommend just any book. You can assist parents and church school teachers by recommending books containing beneficial Bible stories. You can censor books containing stories which could damage little children. And you can provide information about child development to parents to assist them in using their Bibles as resources to find appropriate stories and verses. No doubt you are more thoroughly acquainted with the Bible than I am. It is a part of your preparation for your professional career as a religious educator. The best way I can help you at a theoretical level is to review developmental levels and the principles of effective attitude education. I will give practical illustrations, but you will still have the major task of integrating information and educating parents in how they can best use the Bible as a resource.

DEVELOPMENTAL LEVELS

In the following descriptions of developmental levels, I will be focusing particularly on children's beliefs about God and Jesus because the Bible as a resource is rich with stories about God and Jesus. You may want to review the descriptions of developmental levels in the chapters on faith, hope and love to give you a more complete picture. I will be moving on to the educational goals for faith, hope, and love in a later section of this chapter.

Newborn and Infancy. I combine these two levels not because they are unimportant, but because the Bible has no meaning to the baby. God and Jesus have no meaning because they are not seen. Only toward the end of infancy does object constancy begin. Perhaps mature infants know that the Bible is a special book and is not to be touched.

Mature infants may know how to say the words "God" and "Jesus," but remember, babies are busy sorting out parents, siblings, grandparents, a few family friends, and those sometimes frightening strangers. God and Jesus have not yet been distinguished. On the other hand, preschoolers' beliefs about God and Jesus are strongly influenced by the amount of trust in parents that is developed in babyhood.

Toddler. The Bible can have meaning to toddlers. Toddlers can recognize the Bible as a physical object. The older toddlers can begin to learn how they must behave in relation to the Bible if they are to please their parents. The words "God" and "Jesus" can be spoken and associated with a very vague understanding that they are somehow special. Very simple stories from the Bible are appreciated, particularly if they are accompanied by pictures for children to see. Stories with flannelgraph illustrations are excellent so that children can feel as well as hear and see. This is still the sensory-motor stage. Toward the end of toddlerhood, a sense of possession is attained. What belongs to the child and what belongs to others is understood. Now is the time for the children to have Bible storybooks of their own.

The toddler months are filled with fears and frustrations as the struggle between dependency and autonomy is waged. At this time when the very rudimentary beliefs about God and Jesus are formed, I would strongly recommend that stories and verses be not only simple but joyous and happy. Early exposure to the Bible should not introduce materials that are frightening to children or that are so complex that they frustrate. I have stressed the positive particularly in reinforcement because in attitude education the positive approach is more effective in the long run. Now I stress the positive for yet another reason. Children, who are unable to reason as adults do, deserve to be introduced to religion, particularly to God and Jesus, with a positive attitude. Learning to trust their parents to take care of them is still so important that obviously the story of Abraham about to kill his son, Isaac, is inappropriate and even harmful. Help parents to understand developmental levels so that parents learn to use the Bible effectively as a resource.

Runabout. This could be called the "age of magic."[1] Imagination is not only a possibility, it soars. Curiosity knows no bounds. Ask parents how many questions they encounter in one day, any day. Parents can also tell you about imaginary playmates who are very real for their children. Runabouts cannot make the distinction between real and make-believe. And they should not be expected to make that distinction. They do not yet have sufficient cognitive structure. More experience and action are necessary.

God and Jesus can be very real for these children even though God and Jesus cannot be seen. They are imagined. Usually God is imagined to be like the parents. Jesus is imagined to be like a nice family friend. However, the variations are endless. With few exceptions, God is pictured in human form.

"God is in my heart," said a four-year-old girl.[2] This may sound like profound religion. It is more likely that Lisa imagines a little man in a box in her chest. Or it may be that Lisa is merely repeating something her parents told her. A more typical remark is Devon's. "I like God. He made our church. Isn't it big! He must have had a lot of bricks."

Any parent will confirm the fact that kids say the most amazing things. What is more amazing is the fact of their faith in things they cannot possibly understand. God is because their parents say so. They need no other reason because they cannot reason. Magic is real. God and Jesus are real.

Actually, this is a marvelous beginning if parents can understand and take advantage of their opportunities for attitude education. They are their runabout's heroes and they model God for their children. These children need their parents' love and guidance just as we need God's love and guidance through Jesus Christ. Children's simple faith in God should be based on positive attitudes about God's love and care for all. Positive attitudes about Jesus as a friend and guide are needed. Negative attitudes about God and Jesus are damaging during this stage of magic.

It is confusing to preschool children to have God presented as a judge who metes out punishment. Children at this developmental level do not understand right and wrong the way adults do. They know when they have been naughty, but only in the sense that their behavior was not approved by their parents. Parents are the sole authority. Parents provide the house or apartment where the children live. Parents provide their food, clothes, and toys. It is parents whom these little ones must please. This they understand. It is overly confusing to expect them to want to please God or Jesus. That will come later. You can help parents to understand this age of magic and parental authority by persuading them to avoid adult concepts such as sin, judgment, and hell as they use Bible stories and verses to expose their children to God and Jesus. Help parents to use Bible stories which promote positive attitudes about God and Jesus, attitudes about love and friendship.

On Beyond. Hopefully, preschool children will reach this most mature level of development before they start school. Unfortunately, many do not. They make the change from home to school ill-prepared for this first transition into the world. (Subsequent transitions occur when they set off to high school and later, when they enter the world of work.)

Step-by-step attitude education as described in this book can certainly help in the progression from developmental level to developmental level. However, it cannot assure that children will reach the level of On Beyond before first grade. Children are unique and some take more time to mature than others. However, if parents have been consistent in their attitude education, if they have followed the eight principles of reinforcement, uniqueness, research, assessment, progression step-by-step, goal setting, building on strengths and stimuli, chances are good that this developmental level will be reached before full days at school begin.

What are the characteristics of On Beyond children? I have spoken of them before. They are: (1) children can make the distinction between make-believe and real; (2) children have discovered that their parents are not perfect and that attention must be given to other authority figures; and (3) children want to belong to a peer group. Hopefully, parents will have a year or two before first grade to reinforce and strengthen the attitude education they have begun. When their children go out into the world of school, they will need a firm attitude base in religion as they face new challenges and frustrations.

These mature preschoolers are still in the preoperational stage of cognition. They think without logic. They think intuitively. Magic as reality is still with them. Their concept of God and Jesus has not changed drastically yet, although inevitably it soon will. Parents should be encouraged to continue to promote positive attitudes of love, friendship, and guidance associated with God and Jesus.

FAITH, HOPE, AND LOVE

Next, I will give you illustrations of parents trying to help their children reach the educational goals for faith, hope, and love through the use of the Bible. You will recall that this is a step-by-step process involving goal setting, adaptations to the unique child, and reinforcement of desired behavior. I will not repeat assessment of developmental level for any particular educational goal. I will confine myself to the Runabout level in the following illustrations of Bible stories or verses in order to focus on the methodology of using the Bible. You can then apply the methodology to other developmental levels.

Faith: The Child Can Learn to Trust the Dependability of the Parent.

Lynn had been sick for several days and was becoming downcast. Her father wanted to cheer her up and reassure her that her parents were helping her to get well again. He told Lynn this story.

"Once there was a father by the name of Jairus. Jairus wanted to help his daughter get well again. He believed that Jesus could help just like Mommy and I believe that the doctor is helping you with the medicine you are taking. Jairus went to find Jesus because he was so sure that Jesus could make his daughter well again. When he found Jesus he begged him to come to his house and heal his daughter. Jesus was glad to help, and he and Jairus set off down the crowded street. It took a long time getting to Jairus's house because there were so many people in the street who wanted to see Jesus. By the time they got to the house, the little girl was even sicker. Jairus was very sad, but he was sure Jesus could help. Jesus took the little girl's hand and kindly said, 'Child, arise.' Jairus had done the right thing in getting Jesus because the little girl got up and was well again. Everyone was very happy."

That is a story from Luke, chapter 8:40–56. The father adapted it for a particular child, at a particular developmental level. Lynn is at the age of magic so that a miracle story causes no problems. Miracles are real. Jairus's daughter was twelve years of age, but no harm is done in changing her age to Lynn's age and personalizing the story for Lynn. The father left out the part of the story where the girl dies. There is no point in introducing the possibility of death to sick Lynn. The messages of the story, Jairus's belief and Jesus' help, are retained. Lynn has received the message that her parents are doing their best to help her. She can depend on them. If she smiles after the story, her father will hug her as reinforcement. Lynn has also received the message that Jesus is a helper.

Faith: The Child Can Learn to Appreciate Nature

Eddie was planning to plant his little vegetable garden and his mother wanted him to plant his seeds carefully. Here is Eddie's Bible story.

"Jesus was a great storyteller. People came from all over to hear him tell a story. He told a story about a farmer who was planting his vegetable garden just as you will be doing. The farmer plowed his field very carefully so that the good soil would be just right for his seeds. But then the farmer in Jesus' story got careless. He let some of the seeds fall on the path. Other seeds he tossed upon some rocks. There were some weeds along the edge of the field, and some of the seeds got among the weeds. Do you know what happened to that farmer's seeds, Eddie? People walked on the seeds in the path, and birds also came and ate them up. The seeds among the rocks couldn't put down roots, and so they dried up. The weeds choked the seeds in the weed patch. The farmer was lucky, though. Some of the seeds did get into the good soil in his field, and they put down roots and grew into wonderful vegetables."

Of course, Eddie's mother elaborated on Luke 8:4–8. She adapted the story to Eddie and personalized it. She left out Jesus' explanation of the parable. Preschool children have no way cognitively to understand parables as adults do. However, they can understand the story if it has a direct relationship to their own experiences.[3]

Faith: The Child Can Have Faith in the Predictability of Events.

Four-year-old Devon went to nursery school three mornings a week. On these mornings he was never ready when it was time to leave the house. His father wanted to help Devon to be prepared.

"I have a Bible story for you, Devon, which may help you get ready for nursery school. It is called 'Noah's Be-Prepared Story.' Do you remember last week when it rained so hard that part of the back yard was covered by water? That was a flood. Now, God liked Noah very much. God also knew that there was a huge flood coming, much, much larger than the one in the back yard. God wanted Noah to be prepared for the flood. So God told Noah to build a great boat that would float on top of the water and save Noah and his family from the flood. Noah believed God, and he worked very hard building the boat so that he would be prepared for the flood . . . ."

The story continued to its happy ending. There was a picture of Noah's Ark for Devon to see. The story emphasized throughout, "Be Prepared!"

I have given you illustrations for the first three educational goals, the ones related to *faith*. There are four more goals: two for *hope* and two for *love*. It is useful here to pause and reflect. First, I want to reinforce what you have just learned from the first three illustrations about methodology or strategy. Admittedly, I made up those stories, not Lynn's father or Eddie's mother or Devon's father. However, I have illustrated a method for using the Bible as a resource. My second reason for reflection at this point is related. Within the confines of this book, space limits me to *introduce* you to new methodologies for religious education. If you reflect now, *you* can repeat the process on your own after the last four illustrations.

What was it that I did in those three stories? It is obvious what I did *not* do. I did not portray parents reading the Bible to their children. I am saying here that using the Bible as a resource for stories is not necessarily reading the Bible to little children. That seems straight-forward, even simplistic. Nonetheless, your experience with parents quickly reminds you that all too often your suggestions that parents use the Bible as a resource are actually interpreted as meaning "read the Bible to your children."

I did attempt to portray parents' thinking about Bible stories, choosing stories that were appropriate for their unique child and then adapting those stories. The term "adapting" Bible stories causes difficulties, I know. Some religious educators would refuse to consider any changing of scripture. Some would allow some omissions. Some would allow elaborations. Perhaps a few would allow distortion of facts (Jairus's daughter's age). I omitted, I elaborated, and I distorted because I am a developmental psychologist. As a developmental psychologist, I did the best I could for Lynn, Eddie, and Devon.[4] On the other hand, as a believing Christian I do not believe that I subverted the meaning of God's word. What I did was to "filter" it. My attempt is to encourage your vision for what religious education can mean for preschoolers so that you can help those children's parents. If you can help parents achieve the filtering process by teaching them about developmental levels, then you can succeed in helping them to use the Bible effectively as a resource. Once teachers realize that preschoolers do not think like adults, then they can appreciate what I have called a filtering process. Filter out what the little children have no way of understanding. They have enough problems adjusting to our world without expecting them to understand religion. I see no reason for rushing them, intimidating them, confusing them, or frightening them. Yet, in the past, religious educators have done these things. Psychologically, it does not make sense.

I dealt only with the Runabout level. You might take the Toddler level yourself; think of a particular toddler and choose a story from the Bible for each of the first three educational goals. First, think of a particular goal appropriate to the developmental level which that unique child can achieve. Choose a Bible story. Adapt the story to the child, personalize and filter the story to match the child's understanding. Plan for the behavior which indicates that the goal has been reached and plan the ways you can reinforce that behavior. Then, proceed to the last four illustrations and repeat the exercise.

Hope: The Child Can Have a Positive Attitude Toward Life.

Jennifer was a happy little Runabout. Her parents wanted to further encourage Jennifer's good feelings about life. One evening when they had finished supper, there was still time for a family get-together before Jennifer's bedtime. Mother, father, and Jennifer discussed all the good things that had happened that day. Jennifer's mother said, "We are all feeling so good. I know a song from the Bible which people sang as they went to their church. I am going to read that song as we look at this picture of all the happy people." Jennifer's mother read the first seven verses of the 95th psalm: "O come, let us sing to the Lord; let us make a joyful noise. . . ." Her goal was to inspire Jennifer with happiness and thanksgiving to God. She knew Jennifer would not understand all the words. However, the beauty of the words and the feelings of happiness in this intimate moment with her parents were understood in Jennifer's own way. After the psalm, Jennifer's face glowed. Her father took her hand and said, "I will go upstairs with you and put you to bed. If you like, I will read the psalm again for you as you are going to sleep."

Hope: The Child Can Learn to be Joyful about Learning.

Cathy was always asking questions. Cathy's mother sometimes got tired of answering questions because Cathy did not always listen to the answers. Her mother told her the story of the boy, Jesus, in the temple: Luke 2:41-52.

"When Jesus was a little boy he asked questions, just as you do. One day, his parents took him to a big city where all the people went to a huge church. It was a church celebration, and that is why people had come from near and far. After the celebration, people started on the way home, but Jesus' parents could not find him because of the crowds. They finally did find him, and guess what he was doing? He was asking questions. The church was very important to Jesus, and he wanted to learn all that he could. There were many teachers in the church. Jesus's parents found him with the teachers, asking questions and listening to their answers. The teachers were amazed by Jesus' questions. They were particularly amazed at how hard he listened to their answers. Jesus was learning so much. Finally, it was time to go home and Jesus went home with his mother and father. 'And Jesus increased in wisdom and in stature and in favor with God and man.'"

Love: The Child Can Begin to Have a Positive Self-Regard.

Mark was short for his age and had difficulty because he was so short. Here is Mark's Bible story of Zacchaeus (Luke 19:17), adapted and filtered for Mark's level of understanding.

"Wherever Jesus went the crowds gathered because everyone wanted to see and hear Jesus. The crowds made it hard for Zacchaeus because he was not very tall. Zacchaeus wanted to see Jesus very much. Do you know what he did? He knew the road Jesus would be taking, and he rushed ahead and climbed up into a tall tree. Here he could look down and see Jesus. When Jesus passed the spot, he looked up and saw Zacchaeus in the tree. Jesus understood how much Zacchaeus wanted to see him and why Zacchaeus had climbed up in the tree. Jesus stopped and called out to Zacchaeus, 'Zacchaeus, make haste and come down, for I must stay at your house today.' My, how good that made Zacchaeus feel. He felt like a million dollars as he came down out of the tree. He and Jesus went off together for supper at Zacchaeus's house. Jesus made him feel important."

Love: The Child Can Begin to Have a Positive Orientation to Others.

What better story for Karen than Jesus feeding the 5,000 (John 6:1–14). She was beginning to do helpful things for other people. When the family had guests, Karen could help by passing the food.

"Once there was a little boy who wanted to see Jesus. The people had heard that Jesus would be coming to their village. An uncle promised to take the little boy. His mother packed a picnic lunch for the little boy. They went together to the hill where Jesus was talking with the people. The boy saw Jesus and heard his stories. Jesus was so kind the little boy loved him right away. He was intent on listening to Jesus, and he forgot all about the lunch his mother had made for him.

"Jesus' friends were worried because there were so many people listening to Jesus, and they hadn't had anything to eat all day. They asked Jesus what to do. One of Jesus' friends said: 'There is a little boy here who brought a picnic lunch, but I am sure it is not enough to feed all the people.' Jesus told the people to sit down. The little boy came up to Jesus and said to him, 'Jesus, here is the lunch my mother packed for me. You may have it.' Jesus took the lunch, said a blessing of thanks to God, and then he turned to the little boy and asked, 'Will you help me pass out the food to all the people?'

"You can be sure that the little boy was only too happy to help Jesus. They passed out the food and there was plenty for everyone."

SUMMARY

As religious educators, you can assist parents in learning a methodology for using the Bible as a resource in the attitude education of their little children. The steps in this methodology are:

1. Parents should thoroughly understand developmental levels of early childhood. It may be more realistic to

expect their knowledge for just one category of development at a time such as for faith, hope, or love, or for beliefs in God and Jesus. 2. Parents should assess their child's level of development so that they can gain a sense of future possibilities at the succeeding level. 3. Parents should evaluate their unique child's specific needs within the family situation and set a goal for their child. 4. Now, parents can go to the Bible to find a story or verse which is appropriate. 5. The next step is to adapt the story for their unique child. They should personalize and filter the story to match their child's understandings. 6. Parents should tell the story or read the verses. 7. Reinforce desired behaviors. Your task as religious educator is to teach parents the above steps and, above all, to help them to understand and appreciate developmental levels.

Furthermore, you can:

1. Recommend appropriate storybooks of Bible stories. 2. Urge your parents not to tell stories by reading out of the Bible. Adapt stories to the unique child. 3. Avoid stories with negative or frightening content. Preschool children need happy, joyful stories as they first learn about God and Jesus.

Chapter 10

Prayer

In the last chapter on the Bible, I focused on the family and whatever takes place concerning the Bible in homes. I will retain that focus in this chapter on prayer. It is obvious that the older preschool children will encounter the Bible and prayer when they go to church. The same points that I make about the Bible and prayer in the home apply to methods used to teach the little ones about the Bible and prayer at church. However, I am moving from a home-centered use of resources out into the world. The church will be reserved for the later chapters. Now, the focus is still on how you can help parents at home.

I like the dictionary definition of prayer as "communion with God and a recognition of his presence." I do not like definitions that contain "urgent plea," "beseeching earnestly" or "reverent petitions," at least not when teaching little children about prayer. My reason, of course, is that teaching little children about prayer is attitude education. I maintain that for preoperational children religious education is attitude education, nothing more and nothing less. Beyond that, for attitude education to be effective, some attitudes are appropriate and some attitudes are inappropriate. If a prayer is an "urgent plea" or a "reverent petition," or if praying is "beseeching earnestly," children may learn inappropriate attitudes which may be overly confusing. I will be explaining shortly. First, I want to establish the definition of "communion with God and a recognition of his presence" as related to appropriate attitudes for children to learn.

"Communion with God and a recognition of his presence" is a very broad definition. It is on the level of an abstract generality. The specificities of what kind of communion and how to recognize his presence are not spelled out. "Urgent plea," "reverent petition," and "beseeching earnestly" are much more specific. In fact, they are too specific. I am making the point about generalities and specificities on purpose. Let me explain.

The basis for the "new math" was the startling discovery that children's natural way to learn mathematics was to start with the abstract generalities and work forward to the concrete specifics.[1] They can grasp generalities about numbers even if only intuitively. It is more difficult, in fact with preschoolers it is impossible, for them to start with the multiplication tables and with the other mechanics of addition, subtraction, and division and generalize given those specifics. Even though it may seem backward to adults, the natural way children learn mathematics is to start with generalities.

I submit that in religious attitude education about prayer, this rationale should be followed. Start with the generalities of prayer and work forward to the specifics. The following figure lists the categories commonly associated with prayer.

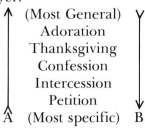

(Most General)

Adoration

Thanksgiving

Confession

Intercession

Petition

(Most specific)

A   B

I have arranged the categories so that from top to bottom they read from most general down to most specific (or least general). I am afraid that in the past we religious educators have tended to start children with petitionary prayers and have worked up, as in line A, through intercession, confession, thanksgiving and finally adoration. Or they have tended to teach all kinds of prayers with no regard to any line of progression.

Preschool children are being introduced to prayer for the first time. I believe that line B demonstrates the best line of progression. Start with adoration and gradually work down the levels of specificity. Furthermore, I recommend that the progression go no further than thanksgiving with preschool children. In effective attitude education, confession, intercession, and petition are inappropriate. Children are being introduced to God. Why run the risk of negative results in their attitudes toward God? I will explain.

PETITION AND INTERCESSION

Little children are egocentric. They want what they want immediately. When they ask God for something and do not receive it, in their eyes God becomes mean and stingy. Let Santa Claus receive petitions. Somehow or other most children recover from disappointment in Santa Claus without too much trauma. Most do mature and understand Santa Claus as the "spirit of giving." Nonetheless, I see no reason to risk misunderstandings and distortions with such an important concept as God. It is better to concentrate on adoration and gratitude.

Intercession is another matter of concern. If children are taught to pray for Aunt Helen who is sick and Aunt Helen dies, what effect will that have on children? The risk here is that a bad God did not help Aunt Helen or that a nasty God took Aunt Helen away. That risk can be avoided by teaching only the positive attitudes of adoration and gratitude in prayers for a preschooler.

There are two other areas I wish to deal with because of the risk factor involved. The first has to do with a component of petitionary prayer. There are some religious educators who advocate prayers for little children that are petitions for God's comfort and strength. God's comfort and strength are adult concepts. Comfort and strength to children come from parents. The connection to God is much too abstract for children. How terrible to teach children to pray, "If I should die before I wake . . . ." That is an extreme but common example. Another one goes something like "God please protect me from all monsters, bogeymen, hurts, and pain." The emphasis of these kinds of prayers is on fears. That is far from a positive attitude about praying. Fears are better handled by teaching the attitudes that were presented in the chapter on hope.

These kinds of prayers also run the risk of placing God again at a disadvantage in children's eyes. When these prayers are unanswered, God is less than a success to children. The fears remain; God has failed. I do not think it is necessary to run this risk.

CONFESSION

Some religious educators advocate that little children should confess in prayer their so-called "sins." I do not agree. The rationale of these educators is that children feel guilty about their wrongdoings. They will be comforted by asking for God's forgiveness. You are dealing here with some false assumptions. True, children are aware of their wrongdoings. However, to assume that they have sinned is quite beside the point. Wrongdoings are no more than engaging in socially unacceptable behavior, unacceptable to adults, that is. When behavior is examined from the children's point of view, the "sin" label disappears. To brand children further with guilt before God is a gross disservice to children. The risk here is that children will perceive God as a harsh judge who metes out punishments. The assumption that children have any understanding of sin is all wrong. It is impossible for them to conceive of sin as adults do. The idea that they will feel comforted by God's forgiveness is another unrealistic expectation.

Children feel comforted by their parents' forgiveness. Children want discipline from their parents, not from God. Forgiveness and discipline are here and now to children. They should not be burdened with having to relate the realities they must deal with day by day to some "man in the sky." Their first need in religious education is to learn attitudes such as those dealt with in chapters 4, 5, and 6 on faith, hope, and love. You do not need to be in such a hurry about teaching preschoolers all about prayer. Deal with just that segment which can be meaningful to them: adoration and thanksgiving. Put off for later those components of prayer which are high risk at the preoperational level of cognitive structure.

ADORATION AND THANKSGIVING

Having dealt with the caveats, I will move on to what exactly you should teach little children about prayer. How do you teach the attitudes of adoration and thanksgiving? The stimulus of parent role models is powerful. Most children cannot resist a grace of thanks before a meal. I like the Beecher blessing model myself with members of the family holding hands. Most children cannot resist the model of parents' kneeling by the crib and giving thanks. Parents can begin before language is understood. The action of the loved model is powerful.

Language is not as important as the adult model in attitude education. In fact, I would point out that words are hardly important at all, especially for infants and toddlers. The runabouts can learn and memorize prayers and blessings. However, memorized prayers may become jingles and rhymes to the child, obscuring a prayerful attitude. At best, attitudinally, small children conceptualize prayer as talking to an important, magical "somebody." The magic in time is replaced by the mystery of faith.

Thus, grace at meals and nighttime prayers are concrete opportunities to introduce children to praying, particularly if parents model talking with God rather than reciting jingles. However, there is a more subtle method. There are numerous opportunities every day for parents to pause a moment and, with the children, say, "Thank you, God, for the beautiful daffodil," or "Thank you, God, for the peaceful snow," or "The stars and the moonlight are beautiful—thank you, God." Children receive the stimulus of parents' awe, adoration, and thankfulness. The close moment between parents and children reinforces. A moment of religious attitude education at its deepest meaning has been enacted.

FAITH, HOPE, AND LOVE

Prayer has been defined very generally as "communion with God and a recognition of his presence." Attitudes relating to adoration and thanksgiving have been recommended as appropriate in introducing prayer to preschool children. Now, I will inspect the educational goals for faith, hope, and love and discuss how prayers can be used as a resource in achieving those educational goals.

I reviewed developmental levels concerning children's beliefs in God in the previous chapter on the Bible. Therefore, description of developmental levels will not be repeated here. You may want to review the previous descriptions before plunging into the educational goals for faith, hope, and love.

EDUCATIONAL GOALS

1. Faith: The Child Can Learn to Trust the Dependability of the Parent.

Ultimately, the goal of religious education is trust in the dependability of God. Yet, for preschool children that is an unrealistic goal. However, the first step toward trust in the dependability of God is trust in parents. Parents model God to their children, at least until the most On Beyond level of development when children begin to recognize that their parents are not infallible. As educators, you must take children where they are. You must deal with what they can understand. Can parents use prayer as a resource to teach fundamental attitudes for faith? At the very general level of adoration and thanksgiving, prayers are a natural. Children adore their parents if the parents are worthy of adoration. Parents must attend to their own worthiness. At the same time, parents can teach their little children prayers of gratitude for parents. The most simple model for toddlers would be:

1. Parents read from a picture storybook about mother and father animals caring for their babies.

2. Parents suggest a prayer, "Thank you, God, for mothers and fathers."

This simple model can be expanded as children mature. Runabouts can deal with the many ways their parents help them. On Beyond children can be challenged not only by how parents help them, but also by how they can help their parents. The stimulus would include a prayer to God in thanksgiving for parents. The reinforcement would be some sign of parents' approval when children join in with a prayer.

I have given you an apparent model of story and prayer. You undoubtedly can think of other ways besides a story to open the door for an opportunity to introduce a prayer. I will introduce other models as other educational goals are inspected. Opportunities must be chosen which match the developmental level of children with the stimulus and which are adapted to the children's uniqueness. Parents must research each of their children. They must proceed one step at a time so that goals are realistic. They must build on strengths and adhere to the positive. Finally, they must appropriately reinforce any progress.

2. Faith: The Child Can Learn to Appreciate Nature.

I am confident that by now you will have little difficulty with appreciation of nature. You may want to review the one-step goals under this educational goal at the end of chapter 7. An appreciation of nature has been referred to in the chapter on the Bible. I will point out that moments of appreciation of nature are opportunities to encourage through prayer the attitudes of appreciation of God and gratitude for the wonders God has provided. Parents do not necessarily need stories; just those everyday moments when parents and children experience beauty together are preludes to prayer. The sight of a new flower, the first snow of the season, a sunset, or a tiny bird are opportunities for awe which can be used by parents to introduce a prayer of adoration and thanksgiving.

3. Faith: The Child Can Have Faith in the Predictability of Events.

For this educational goal, you can teach parents to use opportunities in their everyday family life. The model in its simplest form is event-prayer-reinforcement. Events can be used both after the fact and before the fact. Here are some examples: After the fact: Kim has just awakened from her afternoon nap. She is rested and happy. Her father says, "Thank you, God, for times to rest. Naptime makes Kim ready to go outside and play." Before the fact: Mike and his family are planning a trip to the zoo. Everyone is looking forward to a good time. They have all planned the trip together. Mother pauses and prays, "Thank you, God, for making our trip to the zoo possible." As children mature, this simple model can be expanded. Stories about the seasons, weather, health care, cooperation, or being prepared can introduce prayers. Wall charts and posters open further opportunities. Once parents get the idea of using opportunities to introduce prayers, they will have many practical suggestions of their own.

4. Hope: The Child Can Attain a Positive Attitude toward Life.

A positive attitude toward life and thanksgiving to God can be related through the kind of informal prayers I have been discussing. Again, it is a matter of alerting parents to opportunities. When children show signs of good feelings toward life, these can be reinforced by parents' prayers of adoration and thanksgiving.

Once more I recommend that prayers not be used in connection with fears and frustrations for the reasons I gave at the beginning of this chapter.

5. Hope: The Child Can Learn to be Joyful about Learning.

Prayers of adoration and thanksgiving can be used to reinforce purposiveness, persistence, and creativity, depending upon children's developmental level (see chapter 5).

Prayers can also be used to celebrate all the wonderful things to learn which God has provided. Appropriate opportunities will be unique for each family and for each child. Parents must learn about appropriate opportunities by researching their own situation and their own unique children.

6. Love: The Child Can Begin to Have a Positive Self-Regard and

7. Love: The Child Can Begin to Have a Positive Orientation to Others.

You may want to review the developmental levels described in chapter 7 on love. As children mature they give up much of their egocentricity and orient themselves more toward others. Their own positive self-regard should remain inact as they make the shift from self to others. Parents will be thankful to God as these maturations occur. Their thankfulness can be shared with their children, thus encouraging the children's thankfulness. The rough model we have used in the previous pages still applies.

1. The opportunity occurs to introduce a prayer.
    A. Parents contrive an opportunity by a story, picture, wall chart, etc.

or

B. The parents seize an opportunity occurring naturally.
2. Parents offer a prayer of thankfulness or adoration. The prayer is adapted to the children and to the children's level of development.
3. Parents reinforce any prayerful behavior on the part of the children.

CONCLUSION

I would like to conclude this chapter on prayer with some quotes from children and their parents. I do this in order to give you real-life examples to enrich what I have said. I also do this in order to encourage your reflection.

The quotes come from reports parents have written who were using the Research Curriculum from the Union College Character Research Project. I have arranged them by the age of the children.

Two Year Old Boys and Girls

Now she insists that we fold our hands, bow our heads, close our eyes, and pray before each meal. She looks to make sure our eyes are closed and then she says the grace. She does very well.

She usually asks to say blessing every evening and always remembers to say prayers at bedtime. Prays for God to bless the various members of the family and whoever she has seen or thought of during the day—including her dog and Big Bird.

He is very anxious to "pray his prayer" at each meal. We were surprised at the originality expressed along with a "sing-song" grace he picked up from his brother. He includes events of the day that he shows appreciation for.

She is conscious of prayer—never allows the family to forget the grace at mealtime. She is quite insistent that we be all ready with hands folded "just so"!

She addresses God in her prayers, but is unable to say what God means to her. "Prayer is for saying 'thank you' for nice things and happy days," she says.

Has offered family prayers before meals. She bows her head and says, "Jesus is a good boy" or "Jesus loves little children." This is learned from older girls when looking at a book. She loves to say, "Amen."

We introduced prayer before meals the summer before we started these lessons. When Daddy was absent from the meal, I would say, "Thank you for the good food, Amen," and he would repeat the last three words. A few days later, we were podding lima beans together. He closed his eyes, with beans in hand, and said, "Good food." Need I say my eyes were wet! Believe he has sensed prayer, but not that we are talking to God.

He is eager to fold his hands and bow his head while Daddy asks blessing; in fact, if he's slow to put down his toys, he's afraid Daddy will go ahead without him and he'll be left out. He never forgets saying grace; his hands fold almost automatically as soon as he is seated.

We took a walk but saw nothing new. When we got back he stayed outdoors for a while and got in the mud. Prayer that night: "Thank you, God, for mud."

Three Year Old Boys and Girls

So far she formulates her own prayer which usually consists of a "Thank you, God, for . . . (and then a long list of all the things on the table) Amen."

Says prayers at night and will add voluntarily from time to time some such remark as, "Thank you for Budge coming to see us."

At one time she couldn't say grace. We then suggested taking turns saying grace with each member making up his own. In this way, she became interested and in a short time was saying a blessing of her thoughts toward God at mealtime.

He thanked God for mothers who made pancakes and French toast and aunts who made waffles (we do not have a waffle iron, so my sister makes waffles for the children when they visit her).

We have been saying grace together. He showed us how the children fold their hands at church. He enjoys doing it. In fact, tonight when we were nearly through dinner, he said, "Let's say that again, Mama." I said, "What?" He said, "Say 'Thank you, God.'" So we did.

Now that she tries to think of something other than food to say "thank you" for, she often seems at a complete loss. Once she said, "Thank you for us and Jesus and for (long pause) hopscotch."

He resented that I was the only one to say grace. He insisted on saying his also. He said, "Thank you, God, for

Daddy. Thank you for Mamma. Thank you for happy boy, John. Thank you for everything. Amen."

Her "Thank you, God" came quite spontaneously. It was apparently introduced at Sunday School. In any event, she simply announced, "I want to say a little prayer" and followed through with "Thank you for the food we eat. Thank you. Amen."

He says his prayers every day. However, he thinks of it more as a fun time than a serious time.

She is now beginning to show some originality in such things as prayers. We have made no attempt to teach any set prayer for either table grace or bedtime. I am glad now that we have not. The children are approaching the idea with such naturalness—really talking to God, which I feel is good. I have used "Thank you, God" in response to her questions about God's plan and feel it is most effective. She evidently feels true reverence for the miracles of nature.

On Tuesday, in his prayer, he thanked God for "the best thing that happened today—the cake." (Angel food, and he ate three pieces.)

Four Year Old Boys and Girls

Insists each of family say grace when we eat. She says, "You first, sister. Say 'Thank you, God.'" Then father and mother and herself last.

He wants to pray. Many times he reminds family to say dinner prayer. Has three prayers for bedtime, and wants all *three* said.

Prayers at night: "Thank you, God, for people, mailman,

postman, milkman, for daddies who have penises and for mothers who can have babies."

Her prayers are quite spontaneous and quite humorous to siblings as well as to parents because they are just as though she were talking to an adult.

Thank you, God, for this food and friends and a happy family.

His prayers are memorized sometimes. Now he is beginning to get away from that and says original prayers. Many times he says silent prayer at night.

He knows that when you pray, you talk to God.

Five Year Old Boys and Girls
Very seldom asks for anything in a prayer; she mostly gives thanks. Some nights she thanks God for her toys and friends. Her favorite prayer:

Thank you, God, for this new day.
Thank you for my work and play.

Last year and now, too, he loves to go to church for the first part of the program and feels very grown up saying the Lord's Prayer with the others.

Likes to sing bedtime prayer, "Father we thank thee for the night."

His evening prayers are often quite original. He almost always thanks God for Jesus and his disciples because of some Bible stories we have read to him.

She addresses God in matter-of-fact way. Uses almost no formal prayer.

Says a prayer and has taught little niece (1½ years old) to pray; this has pleased her very much.

He is adding to his prayers himself, such as "God bless all my nice 'purty' friends all dressed up in their nice good clothes to go to Sunday School."

Chapter 11

Church as Community

"The church communicates its faith by being the community of faith, by offering to
persons an experience of its message."
John H. Westerhoff (1970)

There have been numerous experiments in community
during the last ten years and numerous articles about
community in the literature, of which I am sure you are
aware. Community is quite the "in" thing at present. I
believe in community. However, at least for me, as an
educator and as a psychologist, I want to tighten up definitions somewhat and understand a bit more. The responsible religious educator must ask for theory which informs
methodology.

I believe, at least for the preschool level, that attitude
education is the beginning for a methodology informed by
theory in religious education. In chapter 1, I began by
discussing the headwaters of religious education. Attitude
education was proposed as the way, the only way, to begin
religious education for preschoolers. However, I did identify that headwaters were studied in order to learn about
the whole river. Your ultimate goal as religious educator is
still the mature Christian.

The concept, community, provides a beautiful way to
draw together attitude education, the responsible religious

educator, and the learner in religious education. Therefore, I want to take the opportunity in this chapter to emphasize more strongly some points already alluded to about attitude education, responsibility, and the learner.

"In a church community, participants of all ages love one another, learn together, worship together, and nurture one another in faith."

I deliberately wrote that statement to highlight some mighty ideals. Church as community ultimately models God's community. Heaven on earth is an ideal for which to strive. Nevertheless, that ideal can never realistically be attained. Yet, you can responsibly keep your sights high and use the methods of attitude education as a guide. You can approximate God's community as best you can.

"Theory which informs methodology" can be expanded at this point. As you know by now, I am a Piagetian. Therefore, the person-environment interaction is central to my theoretical statements. At the same time, however, I have struggled to understand the grace of God. I have struggled to understand Christian nurture. I stated in chapter 1 that attitude education is the admixture of the cognitive, behavioral, and affective. I know that religious education has a large component of feeling. I also know that educators must deal with expanding spirals on the part of the learner. As person-environment experiences multiply, the learner can adapt to increasing complexities. Educators must encourage the expansion, not repress the expansion, of the learning spiral. Preschoolers at the magic, intuitive, "prereligious" stage must be encouraged in their first cycle around the learning spiral in religious education. If, somehow, their encounter with church as community can encourage expansion and not deny it, they will benefit. The attitude education for faith, hope, and love, described in this book, gives you a methodology for encouraging expansion. In attitude education, particularly for preoperational children, feelings must be dealt with. However, feelings are dealt with in a systematic, rational way in attitude education. And cognitive growth is encouraged in like manner.

THE PRINCIPLES OF ATTITUDE EDUCATION

In order to clarify further the role of attitude education in community, I would like to return to the eight principles and reorganize them for you. This will allow a more precise definition of the role of attitude education in adults' perception of children and children's perception of community. Here are the eight principles:

1. Recognizing the uniqueness
   of the learner
2. Researching the learner   Understanding
3. Assessing developmental level
4. Proceeding step by step
5. Goal setting   Realism
6. Building on strengths
7. Providing astimulus
8. Providing reinforcement   Means

As you can see, to the right of the list I have clustered the principles. I have labeled the first three principles "Understanding." These three principles are loaded with the "whys" of attitude education. The last two principles are labeled "Means." They are heavily loaded with the "hows" of attitude education. The "Realism" principles contain both "whys" and "hows."

All eight principles interact with each other and are necessary to the total system. As you work with parents, you will want them to be fully aware of and to use all eight principles in teaching attitudes to their children. It would be ideal for all the adults in your church community to understand the complete system. However, this may not be realistic. This reorganization of the principles gives you an understanding of priorities. If you would improve community, you need to help adults to be aware of at least the "Understanding" principles. There can be no community where there is no understanding.

Understanding of early preschool children must come from the adults. Very young children are too immature to understand adults. They are too egocentric in their perceptions. Only the most mature preschoolers can appreciate adults for the adults' sake. Children learn gradually to understand adults. Church as community is an excellent atmosphere for such learning. You may want to inspect the understanding of the adults in your church to see if a community atmosphere is available to the preschool children. If a community atmosphere is not present, you should consider some adult education to improve adults' understanding of little children.

It is essential for the spiritual health of your church that your church be a resource for parents and children. The kind of positive attitude education I have proposed thus far promotes community in the family. However, the child must learn about the world outside the home. The church as community is a natural resource for parents and children.

Unfortunately, some churches are not communities. The adults ignore and reject little children. The adults do not understand little children. Such a church is a poor resource. In fact, parents can hardly be blamed for not attending such a church.

On the other hand, a church which is a Christian community is a rich opportunity for parents and children. A church community such as this is a *unique* resource in our changing society. Do you realize that the church is the one place left to many parents where they can expose their child to all age levels? Nuclear, mobile families isolate children from grandparents and other relatives. Schools further isolate children with their peers and only a few adults. Many teenagers are isolated from meaningful jobs with older employees. Children are cut off in many ways from the wisdom and experience of older people. Older people are cut off from the magic and charm of the youngsters. Yet, all ages come together at church, a last bastion for intergenerational gatherings. Hopefully, your church is a community of all ages.[1]

DEVELOPMENTAL LEVELS

What are the understandings adults must have of little children as a prerequisite for community? I am going to describe the developmental levels again as one way to answer that question. I will be dealing with how children perceive your church's people and what the children's needs are at the various developmental levels.

Newborn and Infancy. Newborns, of course, do not perceive other people as distinct from self. This does not mean, however, that they should not receive the same warm love that parents in the home give to them. If your church has a Crib Room where parents can leave their newborns and youngest infants during church worship, make sure that the persons in charge talk to and cuddle the babies. In other words, make sure that the adults—male or female—are true surrogate parents. In the next chapter on church worship, I will deal with newborns and infants attending services. Nonetheless, I will make the point here that church as community can include newborns and infants.

In describing the Infancy level in relation to development, I would also like to mention two maturations which involve the people in the church community. Toward the end of infancy, (1) the babies discriminate between family and strangers, and (2) the babies are apt to become deeply attached to a parent or both parents. These are both normal developments which potentially can present perils for parents who bring their babies to church. If "strangers" at church force themselves upon the babies, the poor babies may become deeply frightened. Help the people in your community to understand this part of development. Furthermore, if the people in your community attempt to enforce separation of babies and parents and if babies resist, what happens for babies is a reinforcement of separation anxiety. Infants in a church community need free access to their parents at all times.

Toddlers. People as persons other than family become distinguishable. Total strangers can still be frightening as toddlers make more and more discriminations. For example, toddlers can still be frightened by a beard, a bald head, or an aged face, if they have never encountered these before. Also, they have yet to learn that persons outside their family say, "No, you cannot do that." They must learn that people come in different sizes, shapes, and colors. Also, they must learn that there are authority figures other than parents. However, if toddlers are to learn about community outside the family, the lessons should be happy experiences from loving people in your parish. Do whatever you can to protect the toddlers from adults in the church who do not understand little children and who might be harsh and rejecting.

Toddlers are too young to tolerate failures in their initial social contacts outside the family. In a religious community, I do not think you should allow failures. Thus, I say, protect the toddlers. Screen, with the parents, a list of a few in your community who can understand this developmental level. Plan together how contacts can be limited. If you are unable to do this, protect the toddler by advising parents to use the church as a resource as little as possible. The Toddler developmental level does not last more than about twelve months, if the child is not negatively reinforced. Most church suppers or any occasion when large numbers of people gather are overstimulating to most toddlers. Let these little children attain the next developmental level before pushing them into adapting to the church community. Of course, your church community will suffer because of its inability to adapt to toddlers. However, your community is less vulnerable than toddlers. I believe your first responsibility is to the toddlers.

Runabouts. Children at this level of development are not so vulnerable as toddlers. This is a level where I think contacts with the church community are imperative in religious education. If the children are denied contacts with the church community, they are denied a natural opportunity to expand their experiencing of the environment outside their family. The church is, or should be, another base for their learning of religious attitudes. Social experiences with religious persons are involved. To look at the matter the other way around, if the other age levels are denied contacts with runabouts, they are denied a natural opportunity to experience the intuitions and magic of the runabout children. A church community needs both of these experiences in order to be a true community.

I believe that one thing I am apt to do is to paint you a rosy picture and then counter with a string of caveats. That is what comes of being an idealist *and* a realist. My belief in the potential of little children causes me to be an idealist. My realization that adults are filled with human frailties pulls me back to realities. Certainly I know that the Runabout stage is intolerable to many adults. Certainly I know that church suppers, or even worship services, can be ruined by the runabouts. I will be speaking more about these seeming contradictions in the next two chapters.

Right now, as I talk about the generalities of the church as community, I want to focus on opportunities rather than problems.

I have suggested to you that adults can learn from the intuition and magic of runabouts. Now, think, if you will, about the perception of the runabouts as they enter your church community. They expect good things from the people. They expect, for the most part, acceptance and love. They expect respect and consideration. (They would still be at the Toddler level if they did not, and many older preschoolers are still at the Toddler level.) They are still new at giving acceptance and love to others. What an opportunity for the church as community to offer religious education to the runabouts!

Too often the opportunities are not recognized. The people in your community are the resource. What people in particular can be considered as resources and how can you take advantage of potential opportunities?

There is an authority figure in your community who stands out from the rest in the church hierarchy. The priest, pastor, or minister is head person, at least to children as they perceive your community. However, that person is not God for adults, even though many adults put the figure next to God. For runabouts, the authority figure very probably is God. I believe that children need to know personally their priest or minister. At the very least, you can personalize the man (or woman) in the long robe. Get your minister to interact with runabouts.

I see no reason, at this developmental level, to hide from children the act that other persons in the community are on the church team. If children can appreciate a family team which cooperates in getting household tasks done, they can begin to appreciate the team which supervises the running of the church. The church officers are a resource for runabouts. The church officers can be prepared by you for meeting with children of this developmental level.

The community at large, the congregation, is another opportunity. If the runabout's perception of the community at large is unfriendly, unaccepting, even hostile (church is for adults only), you have a large problem. From my perspective as a developmental psychologist, you have got to take measures that may mean educating the members in your community to understand the importance of developmental levels. Specifically, I mean educational groups studying developmental psychology. There is no true community without adults understanding how little children grow and develop.

If educational groups are impossible, I suggest that you

enlist the aid of the minister. Perhaps a sermon on child development and community would help. Perhaps a congregational letter would improve understanding. You can enlist the aid of teachers and church officers to help you spread information about understanding the runabout child. You can impart information in snatched moments at coffee hours, church suppers, or business meetings. One way or another, let adults know that community includes little children and that community must meet the needs of its runabouts.

On Beyond. These children, as I have said before, are a delight. I am talking about a level of development, not an age level. Some children reach this level as early as three, but that is unusual. Some children reach it at four, five, six, or seven years of age. Some never really reach it. They go on to concrete thinking but, unfortunately, their emotional and attitudinal development is imperfect. They do not have a firm basis from the preschool years to prepare them for the buffeting which they must meet in their future life. They are potentially crippled. I say "potentially" because there are recorded cases of seven-year-old abused children who have made remarkable progress when put into a loving environment.[2] These, perhaps are exceptions.

My dramatic appeal to you is (1) to expedite attitude education in the early preschool years so that the children in your community do arrive at the On Beyond level before school entry, and (2) if you have older preschoolers who have not reached this developmental level, strengthen your efforts to improve the church as a resource so that all your little children enter secular school as On Beyond children.

Having said that, I will attempt to focus more sharply on the On Beyond children's perception of the church as community. The markers for this developmental level are, of course: (1) the ability to distinguish between make-believe and real, (2) the recognition that parents are not perfect, and (3) the ability to begin to understand that others do not necessarily feel as they do. Therefore, these children are going to perceive the church as community as (1) filled with make-believe and real and they will wonder how to make distinctions. They will also perceive the church as community by (2) recognizing that the minister, church officers, and teachers may be authorities whom they must decide to trust or not. Finally (3), these On Beyonders will perceive the church community as a laboratory for exploring the feelings and behaviors of others in relation to their own feelings and behavior. I will enlarge upon these points in the next two chapters where I will leave generalities and inspect specific components of church. However, I believe that you should think about these generalities as you ask yourself the question, "Does the church community meet the needs of the On Beyond preschool or school-age children?"

Now, I want to point out some other factors about the On Beyond level which are carry-overs from the Runabout level of development. When I speak about levels of development, as I hope you have appreciated, I do not intend that you think of pigeonholes. I am certainly not suggesting that children can be classified as belonging in this or that box. Development, as far as is known, is not so simple as climbing from Step 1 to Step 2 and forever hereafter Step 1 is done. The psychologists Erickson and Maslow suggest to me a sponge model.[3] Persons can develop up through levels but can always partially drop back to a former level depending upon the holes in their personal sponges.

The other factors I referred to are throwbacks to the former level, the Runabout level. The curiosity about learning is still present. And magical, intuitive, or preoperational thinking is still present. The preschooler mode of thinking is all important in your understanding of how On Beyonds perceive church as community. In these respects, I do not think that I am introducing anything new beyond what I have previously said about the Runabouts. Except that when you put the premises of (1) distinctions between make-believe and real, (2) the possibility of diverse authorities and (3) a laboratory for learning about others up against (a) curiosity and (b) the magical, intuitive, preoperational thinking, you have a real challenge.

FOCUS ON PARENTS

I have spoken thus far from the focus of what you can do to improve the community by helping other age levels understand little children. Now I will change the focus to what you can do to help parents make best use of the resource, church as community. Return to the use of all the eight principles and to the educational goals. However, when discussing community, a concept at a high level of generality is implied. Thus, I am going to address myself only to the educational goals for love which is also at a high level of generality. Community is people. Love involves people. How can parents use community to teach their children attitudes of (1) having a positive self-regard and (2) having a positive orientation to others? (You might want to review chapter 6 on love.)

Parents of Toddlers

I would like to tell you a real-life story at this point. The story is about a three-year-old boy in my church community. I will call him Derry (not his real name). He appeared in the picture with me on the back cover of the book, *Celebrating the Second Year of Life.* I do not know whether his parents have used that book with Derry, but I do suspect that they have enacted the spirit of that book. The family and I are merely acquaintances, although I have been in their home and know that the religious education of Derry is very important. Today, I watched Derry at the Sunday morning worship service. When Communion was about to begin, his mother went to the church school nursery and saw to it that Derry joined in the community worship with his parents. What struck me was the confidence of that small, three-year-old marching up the aisle ahead of his parents to participate in whatever was going on in his community.

I also want to tell you what else I have observed about Derry's family. They were in church frequently when Derry was a newborn. He was baptized in the church in early infancy. Then my memory tells me that I did not see Derry in church, certainly not at church meetings, pot-luck lunches, suppers, or any activities for several months. I was quite sure that he was not in the Crib Room since I did not see his parents in church. Now, at three years of age, Derry and his parents are with us regularly again. And Derry strides down the aisle self-confidently. He feels good about himself and about his church community.

I have told you about Derry to illustrate the sensitive and understanding way the parents use our church in exposing Derry to community. They have understood his development from level to level. They have researched their unique child. Derry is a rather serious little guy who appears to study the situation carefully before jumping in. He is apt to go his own way, do his own thing. I am not suggesting that all parents keep their toddlers away from the church until they are runabouts. I am suggesting that Derry's parents correctly assessed Derry and protected him during shy periods when he needed protection. Now that he is a self-confident runabout, he is ready for the larger community outside his home.

We have other toddlers in our church who stay in the Crib Room during worship services. Some of them are happy, and some are not. I do not think the unhappy toddlers should be there. However, a child like David should be there. David at one and a half years of age is very outgoing. He is constantly reaching out to others and will let anyone pick him up and admire him. In our church, just about everyone does pick up David. He thrives on attention which he gets in abundance. David is easily distracted which helps when he occasionally displays a show of temper. There is usually someone on hand to distract his attention and start him playing happily again.

David's parents are sensitive and understanding. They also are aware that David's needs can be met in our particular church community.

I have illustrated at the Toddler level two things you can offer parents. First, you can help them understand their own unique children. The methodology of using the first three principles of attitude education, the "why" principles, will assist you. The second thing you can offer parents is help in matching their children's unique needs to the church community. This is more subtle. At your church, are children's needs going to be met? Discuss this question with parents.

Derry's parents decided that Derry's needs would not be met by coming to church during the Toddler months. David's parents made the opposite decision for David. Decisions must be made child by child, and you can assist parents in these decisions.

The unfortunate situation occurs when parents do not consciously make decisions about how to use their church as a resource. They assume that of course they should take their children to church. The results from such nondecisions are often some very unhappy little children. Unhappy children in church can be perceived by others as unlovable, particularly when these children act out their frustrations in an aggressive manner. Your community will have problems with unhappy children. Those children are already having problems. Perhaps those problems are better solved at home with your assistance.

Another unfortunate situation is three-, four-, and five-year-old toddlers in the church. Physically, they are very good at running about, but Toddler is still their developmental level. These children are just very slow in maturing or there is something in their home environment or perhaps in the day care center or nursery school that is retarding their development. They can cause mayhem in your church. We have one such child in our church. She kicks and hits other children and even the adults. She darts here and there with no regard for others. Now, our church is a pretty friendly place, but it is very difficult to love Francie. Francie comes from a single-parent home. Even though her mother is infinitely patient and warmly loving, Francie is a horror. Francie's mother is receiving counseling.

If you have a Francie in your church, I suggest that you teach the parents the eight principles of attitude education. My suspicion is that the problem, if it is a problem of retardation of development, correlates with a misuse or misunderstanding of one or more of these principles. I am going to list the principles again, but this time accompanied by common misuses or misunderstandings. This will help you in locating problems and in helping parents to correct the misuse or misunderstanding.

Principles	*Misuse or Misunderstanding*
1. Recognizing the uniqueness of the learner	"Children are all alike."
2. Researching the learner	"It isn't worth the bother."
3. Assessing developmental level	The belief that children are miniature adults.
4. Proceeding step by step	Parents' unrealistic expectations
5. Goal setting	Parents have no systematic approach
6. Building on strengths	Parents try to correct faults
7. Providing a stimulus	Parents ignore opportunities or provide inappropriate stimuli
8. Providing reinforcement	Children lack reinforcement or parents provide inappropriate reinforcement.

Unless you can solve the problems with parents of these older toddlers, you run the risk of damaging whatever community you have in your church. The longer the problem continues, the more damaging it can be to community and the more difficult it becomes to solve. Attack problems as early as possible.

Parents of Runabout Children

Hopefully, most of the three-, four-, and five-year-old children in your church are at least at the Runabout level of development. What can you say to parents of a runabout concerning the development of positive self-regard and a positive orientation to others in the church community?

The most general advice is to encourage parents in their understanding and practice of all eight principles of attitude education. Positive self-regard is enhanced as children learn skills. Some of the most important skills at this development level are interpersonal skills, such as sharing, taking turns, and cooperative play. Community is an excellent place to practice these skills. Runabouts are mature enough to learn these skills. Children are still motivated by self-pleasure. Children are still unaware that others have feelings that differ from their own feelings. Help your parents to be sensitive to successes and failures. Help them to monitor their children's experiences, so that potential problems can be prevented. Help them to set realistic goals and to proceed in very small steps.

Since children at the Runabout level of development seek advice and guidance, demonstrate to parents the effective technique of role playing. These children want to be prepared for coming events. Before the event, parents can act out with their children how the youngsters are to behave at church functions and how others are apt to behave.

Children at all developmental levels will gain a positive

orientation to others if parents take a transitional step between the community of the family and the community of the church. Urge parents to invite the minister, teachers, and other members of the church into their homes. The occasions can be prepared for by role playing. Children can have assigned tasks such as taking coats or passing food. Such responsibilities encourage both positive self-regard and a positive orientation to others.

Parents of On Beyond Children

As children reach the On Beyond level of development, more possibilities in community exist for parents to consider. These children can recognize other people's feelings. True sympathy and concern for others is beginning. Previously children exhibited sympathetic behaviors, but their real concern was for themselves. Kissing a hurt child or parent was soothing themselves lest they receive the hurt. Now, On Beyonds can appreciate that others hurt even though they do not. They are ready to learn skills of sharing sympathy. They are ready to learn skills of sharing love. They are ready to become actively participating members in community. They can learn to initiate concern for others.

Of course, this is only a beginning and parents must proceed step by step, reinforcing all progress. I am going to close this chapter by listing opportunities to share feelings for the On Beyond child in a church community. As you discuss these opportunities with parents, no doubt they will identify other opportunities. Then together you can make plans with parents for using the resource, the church community, so that their children can practice love.

Making new friends.

Delivering the altar flowers on Sunday.

Accompanying parents on sick calls or calls to shut-ins.
Congratulating church members on birthdays.
Helping set tables or waiting on tables at church suppers.
Comforting the lonely or unhappy of all age levels.
Participating in celebrations.
Joining the elderly at worship services.
Adopting a grandparent in the congregation.

Chapter 12

Church Worship

The word, "worship," has roots in an ancient Anglo-Saxon word, "weorthscipe," which means "worthy-ship" or of more worth. Thus, worship has to do with that which is valued. Church worship is the action of acclaiming that which is valued most highly, God.

The word, "liturgy," as you know, comes from the Greek word, "leitourgia." Originally, it meant an action in the service of the community. This meant the building of a temple or a theater or a civic building in the Agora. Religious liturgy down through the ages has come to have two meanings; the word, "rite," expresses the first meaning; the word, "ceremony," expresses the second meaning. A rite is the written words which structure the liturgy. Ceremony is the action part of the liturgy.

Religious education for preschool children is attitude education. Therefore, I prefer the terms "worship" and "ceremony" rather than "liturgy." Preschool children are unable to understand, intellectually, the written words of the rites and it is not important that they understand. What is important is their learning of attitudes from church services. They learn by experiencing, by participating in the actions of worship and ceremony. They learn by worshiping with the community of faith.

In the previous chapter, I discussed church as community. Community is a generalized abstraction which is expressed in differentiated forms in church life. One concrete expression is church worship. The church worship is a form of community in action. A church service is a form of "doing" community.

"DOING" FAITH

In the previous chapter, I linked community, in general, with the educational goals for love, another generalized abstraction. Now I am proposing that worship be linked with the educational goals for faith. In worship, worshipers are participating in community and love by faithing,[1] doing faith. You cannot teach faith. At best, you can teach attitudes for faith. For preschool children, one way to teach attitudes for faith is by allowing children to do faith by joining the loving community in worship. In the church community, the main locus for learning about faith is in the worship service where faithing is experienced. The main locus for learning about hope at church is in the church school. That linkage will be developed in the next chapter.

If I had not approached religious education at the preschool level, the headwaters, I probably would have missed these insights. I probably would be where a great many religious educators are: that is, believing that the purpose of the church school is to teach Christian faith. Since I approach religious education of preschoolers as attitude education, I cannot escape the conclusion that the young learner in the church community learns about faith in the church worship services. This is not to say that preschool children do not learn anything about faith in the church school. They do learn something about faith in the church school. However, in the church community they learn the most about faith by participating in worship services. Pre-operational children learn best by experiencing.

CHILDREN AND THE WORSHIP SERVICE

In some churches, worship services are strictly for adults. The children may be allowed to come in for a short period of time. However, the children are instructed to (1) walk quietly, do not run; (2) do not talk; (3) squeeze into the first two pews; and (4) no hitting, biting, kicking, (no anything except sitting quietly). How can children feel welcome with all the prohibitions and the physical discomfort?

My father was a minister to a large urban parish. The first three pews in Westminster Presbyterian Church in Albany, New York are child-size pews, an obvious clue to the high priority given to welcoming children in the church. The children entered the church during a hymn. They could sit with their parents or they could sit in comfort in the front pews. The order of worship was arranged so that the children were present for a prayer and one of the lessons. Then Dr. Welles came down the chancel stairs and stood with the children for the children's sermon.[2] Both children and adults loved his stories. He never preached object lessons. He never talked down to the children. His stories were about how a hymn was written (the organ would play the hymn), about the seasons of the year, about families, or about the rose window high up over the altar. He often asked for answers to questions or for animal noises or clapping. The entire congregation loved these stories and participated as community in the joy or sorrow, awe or amazement. After the children's sermon, the offering was received while the congregation sang another hymn. The children left during the last verse. You can bet those children felt welcome in that community. They were learning about faith by worshiping in community.

I am aware that few ministers are blessed with the talents necessary for good children's sermons. I am also aware that some congregations go to much greater extremes in welcoming the children. I am going to describe another worship service in a fictional church, putting together a number of ideas for welcoming children in the worship of the community and providing for the children's participation in worshiping or faithing.[3]

Children arrive with their parents at the beginning of the service. They are welcome to stay for the entire service. They may move around freely at any time during the service, although they are discouraged from entering the chancel area except when invited there by the minister. There is a ten or fifteen-minute period in the service when they are invited to join the minister in the chancel. At this time they share with the rest of the congregation their understanding of the lessons, a hymn, or whatever the minister challenges them to speak about. Of course, since this extra time is added to the service, the minister's sermon to the adults is cut down in time accordingly. At the offertory, the children mingle with the congregation offering the pictures they have drawn or flowers prepared before the service. Passing the peace is initiated at each pew by the children. Crayons and paper are available at the back of the nave for children who get tired of long periods of sitting in a pew.

ADULTS' ATTITUDES

Perhaps you can picture and accept the worship service I have just described. I must say I have some difficulties. I do not disagree with any single suggestion. In fact, singly some of the ideas I would heartily endorse. My difficulty has to do with so much change. It would require a great deal of planning to prepare most adults for feeling comfortable with such a service. Such drastic changes may be an excellent long-range goal. However, in short-range planning I do not believe that drastic changes are necessary in most churches. What matters is the atmosphere of the worship service. Atmosphere includes the physical appearance of the church, the sounds in the church, the symbols in the church, and the attitudes of the adults.

Most churches by design are lovely, most churches have organs and stained glass windows, most churches have lecterns, pulpits, altars, and a cross in appropriate locations. I believe that you can take things as they are and build in small changes for influencing the attitudes of adults. There is already so much to offer little children in present worship services and in the physical atmosphere, if you can use the existing opportunities.

I have identified the worship service as part of the religious educator's domain. The learners, even the youngest learners, learn about faith by worshiping. Your responsibility is to change gradually adults' attitudes so that children are welcomed in whatever worshiping they are capable of within the loving community. Adult attitudes are not always changed quickly. Adults are apt to feel strongly about the worship service. Forgive me if I use my own church again as an illustration.

Three years ago we began what was for us a change in the worship service, albeit a small change. The rector decided that we should take "passing the peace" in earnest. The congregation did not object on any logical basis. Yet the rigidity of feelings for the first year or two! We were instructed that on the rector's sign each person sitting on the center aisle seat of a pew would shake the hand of the immediate neighbor and say "Peace." The neighbor would do likewise and so on across each pew. Gradually, we began to loosen up. Attitudes and behaviors began to change. We began to pass the peace, not rigidly, but spontaneously. We no longer shook hands over the heads of children; we included them. Were they surprised! Today, couples get a chance to embrace in church. We pass the peace to those in our pew, to those in the pew ahead of us, and to those in the pew behind us. It gets quite disorderly with hands and arms reaching out every which way. And the children are a part of it.

Other changes were occurring in our community which complemented what was happening with the celebration of the peace of the Lord. Baptism in our community is celebrated at the Sunday morning worship service. The rector asks all of the children to come with him down the aisle to the baptismal font at the rear of the nave. There with the parents, godparents, and families, the children are witnessing and participating in the ceremony. After the rite, the rector with the baby walks up one side of the nave introducing the child to the congregation, up into the chancel for the choir members and back down the other side of the nave so that all of the people can see the new child of our community.

My point is that you can take your church as community where it is right now and logically plan step by step how to make religious education a force in your church. I am proposing that you use the methodology of attitude education as your entree. Your concern in worship is largely attitude education for adults and little children as well. I am proposing that attitude education is an important and distinguishable factor in religious education. Religious educators have long wondered why they have an identity problem. The identity problem has caused all sorts of divisions between the cognitive school and the affective school, between the information-giving teams and the nurture teams, between the theologians and the social scientists, and between the laissez faires and the activists. I am proposing that attitude education is a middle ground. I am proclaiming that attitude education necessarily combines the cognitive and the affective which, it seems to me, are the root difficulties in the other dichotomies. I further suggest that the religious educator identify the problems that can somehow be solved by attention to the attitude education component in religious education; certainly at the preschool level, there is no other effective choice but attitude education. Also, in worship the problems in education can largely be solved by attitude education.

Thus far, I have discussed your role in your church. I have given you my honest opinions from where I stand. I have not reviewed the developmental levels again. You have the knowledge and wisdom to do that yourself. By now, you should know the small child's needs for community within the worship of the church's loving community. If you do not, review the previous chapters in this book. With some review, I believe that you can figure out how I would answer your individual questions.

THE RELIGIOUS EDUCATOR AS MEDIATOR

As I did in the previous chapter, I have looked at your responsibilities as educator in the total "church" picture. I have discussed the integration of your position in the realities of your particular situation. Now I am going to move on to the second area, the aids you can give to parents in using church worship as a resource.

First, I would like to give you a few educated beliefs. To my knowledge, there has been no research in these particular areas, although there should be. I do not know if unhappy children forced to go to church are damaged, but I suspect they are. I do not know how much adults will tolerate from youngsters who disrupt worship, but I suspect the threshold is rather low.

My honest belief, therefore, is that your position is similar to that of a mediator. From my point of view, your first responsibility is to the little children. However, you also have a responsibility to the rest of the congregation. How much can they tolerate? I believe that you should talk over with parents the answers to three questions. The parents ultimately must make the decisions, but you can mediate.

1. Will the unique child get *any* benefit from attending church worship?
2. If the unique child will benefit, are there only certain portions of the worship service where the benefits accrue?
3. Is the unique child *ready* to attend the complete worship service?

My questions are telling you that I think certain children, particularly those unhappy older children who are still at the Toddler developmental level are best ministered to some place else. Of course, it depends upon the child, upon your community and upon what transpires in your worship service. There is the matter of matching child and situation involved here. The matching must be done child by child.

When I refer to matching, I allude to the understanding

principles (uniqueness, researching, and assessment) and to the realism principles (step by step, goal setting, and building on strengths). You can work with parents on these six principles in order to help them to make decisions about their children's attendance at worship in your church and about how much of the worship service is useful.

THE MEANS PRINCIPLES

Now I turn attention to the means principles (stimulus and reinforcement). If you will recall from chapter 7, there were categories of stimuli and categories of reinforcers. The following lists will refresh your memory.

Stimuli	*Reinforcers*
Sensory	Physical
Motor	Verbal
Preoperational Cognitive	Concrete
Intrinsic	Intrinsic

I will have a few words about each of these categories which you may wish to discuss with parents.

STIMULI

1. *Sensory Stimuli.* Turn your mind to the sensory stimuli in a church worship service. I will begin with some examples for each of the five senses but you can complete the examples for your own church.

Seeing: The nave and chancel, the stained glass windows, the people, the procession and recession, the vestments

Hearing: The organ prelude, the hymns, the choir's anthems, the prayers, the creeds, the silences

Touching: Passing the peace, the blessings, baptism, the minister's handshake

Smelling: Flowers, incense

Tasting: The elements

Help parents recognize the potential of sensory stimuli in church worship. It is almost as if the worship service evolved with sensory stimuli in mind for all ages. Sensory stimuli are particularly important for the youngest children.

2. *Motor Stimuli.* Whoever said that a worship service was devoid of motor activity? There are the processional and recessional, there is the passing of communion or going forward to the chancel rail; there is the offering; there is passing the peace; there is standing, sitting, kneeling; there is the activity in the chancel. The trouble is that there is not enough activity directly involving active preschoolers. However, parents can be alert to whatever activity is going on to use as stimuli for their young learners.

3. *Preoperational-Cognitive Stimuli.* Now, examine symbols in a worship service. What are the symbols the children see in a worship service? Again, I will begin a list which you can complete for your church: the cross, the altar, the bread and wine, the minister's robe, people kneeling. The list could go on and on. Anything in worship which stimulates a child to think is a cognitive stimulus. Children's questions give evidence that children have been cognitively stimulated. I believe that parents should answer their children's questions. However, children are at a preoperational level and the adults' answers must match the children's level of understanding. "What is a cross?" needs no explanation of the resurrection. "It stands for Jesus" is sufficient. "What is an altar?" can be answered by "It is a table." Help prepare parents for answers which are direct and simple.

4. *Intrinsic Stimuli.* The possibility of children being intrinsically stimulated by participating in church worship depends upon the pleasure such participation brings to the children. The possibility is excellent if the unique children are well matched to the community's particular worship service. Your worship service should be intrinsically stimulating to all in your community.

REINFORCERS

1. *Physical Reinforcers.* Physical reinforcers are the only reinforcers available for newborns and early infants, of course. However, physical reinforcers are still important for toddlers, runabouts, and on beyonds, judiciously applied. Babies need direct physical contact during worship services. Sometimes, toddlers want a lap to sit on. Other times toddlers resent the limitations of being held on a parent's lap. I have watched toddlers happily exploring within their pew, even exploring within adjoining pews. They are reinforced by parents' smiles, parishioners' smiles, and the contents of adults' handbags. Parents should be alert to situations during worship service when the happy explorer is not greeted by positive reinforcement. When the reinforcement is nonexistent and certainly when it becomes negative, the toddlers should be quickly removed for the children's sake as well as for everyone else's sake. Help your parents to be sensitive to the reinforcers their children are receiving during a worship service. I have pointed out the power of the indirect physical reinforcers (a smile or a nod) in chapter 7. I believe these should be used lavishly during worship for rewarding appropriate worshiping behaviors.

2. *Verbal Reinforcers.* The trouble with verbal reinforcers during worship service is that they must be in whispers, so that other worshipers are not disturbed. Of course, with runabouts and on beyonds, parents can always whisper, "I will talk about that later. But your question is a good one." (Parents should keep their promise.) Delayed gratification with toddlers is not very effective. They need reinforcement immediately. Whispers will have to do except during hymns or other moments when louder sounds will not disturb others. Again, help parents to be aware of disturbance level.

3. *Concrete Reinforcers.* Again, I say, "If it works, use it." Concrete rewards for preschool children are not habit forming if used correctly. I do not approve of parents coming into church with their preschoolers and immediately producing crayons and paper. That does not reinforce any worshiping behavior. I believe that parents and children should enter the church, be seated, and meditate a few moments together. Then, a reward can be given if the children have approximated a meditating behavior. If a physical hug or smile as reinforcement for enjoying the processional is not enough, a concrete reward may be in order. Perhaps the parents are not going to get a great deal out of a worship service with this constant alertness to their children during the hour of worship. Decisions will have to be made whether a physical, verbal, or concrete reinforcer is called for at a given moment. However, I submit that if parents ignore the stimulus-reinforcement system, they will very probably submit themselves to the graver problems of having a "problem kid" in church. With problem children in church, parents are likely to have even less time for their own personal worshiping. I

believe these are questions you should discuss with parents.

4. *Intrinsic Reinforcers.* This level of progress in the religious education of preschool children is an ideal. You cannot accomplish the attainment of this level without the help of parents. Very probably your parents cannot attain this level for their children without your help. It is a goal for you and parents which is possible. On beyond preschool children do exist. Witness these parent reports[4] about their children:

"On Sunday my wife and I were planning to sleep in. Jerry woke us up and said it was Sunday. 'I want to go to church.'"

"Church makes me feel so good!"

"He said, 'I like the choir. When I get bigger I can sing in the choir.'"

These are crude signs of intrinsic reinforcement. They come from only very few children. I present possibilities as your challenge in religious education.

EDUCATIONAL GOALS

Now I will turn from stimuli and reinforcers to addressing the educational goals for faith. Children can learn to:

1. Trust the dependability of parents
2. Appreciate nature
3. Have faith in the predictability of events.

How can you help parents reach these goals given the resource, church worship, in your community?

Trust the Dependability of Parents

This goal has short-range and long-range implications.

The long-range implications have to do with trusting others in your loving community and, ultimately, with trusting God. First, the short-range implications will be inspected.

Infants and toddlers depend on parents to provide creature comforts. They learn to trust parents as these comforts are provided. In terms of a worship service, this means the physical availability of parents in the pew plus some room in the pew to spread out (wiggle room). I believe parents plus one child deserve at least half a pew, if not more.

I would also alert parents that no matter how impressive a sermon is to adults, it very probably is not all that impressive to youngsters. Children can learn to depend upon their parents to provide them with suitable distractions when their attention wanders.

Toddlers particularly can learn to trust their parents to provide them with role models. This is the age of imitation, and toddlers learning worship behavior need a model to imitate. Runabouts will accept coaching and guidance and should receive it from parents during a worship service. Runabouts will welcome such coaching and they will be learning that they can depend on their parents to coach them in acceptable behavior.

The on beyond children have learned that their parents are dependable but not perfect. Now is the time for parents to help their children in decisions about which other authority figures to trust. Here is where your community becomes especially meaningful. Little children can learn to trust the minister and many other adults in the congregation as cooperating with their parents in the guidance of children in worship.

The long-range implications of trust are concerned with

trust in God. Certainly trust in parents and trust in other adults in your church community are steps along the way. You do, however, have to grapple with trust in God on the part of preschool children. Primarily, the trust is in parents, particularly for runabout children. To them, parents are God. However, runabouts and on beyond children, if their religious education has been effective, will also trust a "Santa Claus" God or a magical God. This is perfectly normal and should not be surprising. As a matter of fact, such trust is an excellent beginning. Such trust is the best possible trust for the preoperational child. Remember that the preschool years are only the first swing around on the expanding spiral of religious cognition. During a worship service the term *Father* as applied to God is repeatedly heard by children. It makes good sense to point this out to children if, in fact, the children's fathers are fairly good models for children to image as God. A different situation exists for children whose fathers are not good models. Unfortunately, some fathers are cruel, unloving, unstable, and abusing. My suggestion is that in situations like this you point out to the mothers that they can resist drawing attention to the term Father in worship services or elsewhere but should consider using Jesus as the model of God. After all, that is what the Incarnation is all about.

Appreciate Nature

Appreciation of nature, in the broad sense, is at the core of worship. We thank God for his creation and continual creating of persons, the world, and the universe. Thus, any behavior of awe and reverence, of joy and thanksgiving, are steps toward this educational goal. Parents are apt to miss this broad sense of appreciation of nature, and you may want to draw it to their attention.

When adults think of nature and preschool children,

they tend to think of the out-of-doors, the seasons, grow-ing plants, the mountains, and the weather. That is fine and I have a suggestion for you to pass on to parents: draw parents' attention to the lectionary. In preparation for a Sunday service, they can look up the lessons and the psalm and identify passages about nature. There are some splendid examples, particularly in the psalms. Parents can prepare their older preschoolers to listen for certain pas-sages in the worship service. If the children recognize pas-sages during the service, parents can reinforce.

Have Faith in the Predictability of Events

Church worship services are a natural for children who are learning to have faith in the predictability of events. Services occur at least once every seven days like clockwork. The church calendar is predictable. Every year there is Advent, Christmas, Epiphany, Lent, Easter, and Pentecost, again like clockwork. The liturgy for services is largely predictable. The order of service is predictable. Church worship is a natural way for children to learn to have faith in the predictability of events. Discuss with par-ents the rich opportunities available to them in church worship for exposing their children to predictability. Pre-dictability, dependability, and appreciation are the foun-dations of faith for preschool children. Church worship is an excellent resource for parents to use in teaching their children the foundations for faith.

Chapter 13

Church School

I looked up the word, "school," in the Oxford English Dictionary and I found column after column of definitions. I am going to quote from just one section near the beginning in order to start this discussion.

> Gr. σχολγ orig. leisure, hence employment of leisure, study, and (in later use) a school.

Greek letters are a mystery to me, but the definition of "employment of leisure, study, and a school" is not. My husband and I visited the ruins of the original "Agora" in Athens. Our translation of Agora might be "City Center and Shopping Mall wrapped into one." The Agora was the hub of the ancient Greek city. Here were the municipal buildings and the "Stoa." Rockefeller funds have contributed to a reconstruction of the Stoa of ancient Athens. The Stoa is an awe-inspiring building of classical Greek architecture—columns, symmetry, and space. Imagine a modern "Galleria," our most up-to-date shopping center, done in classical Greek. Imagine a two-storied series of stalls fronting on walkways and endless columns, all opening out to the sky, sun, or stars.

The stalls and colonnades were designed for leisure. Here the accomplishments of the craftsmen were sold. The artifacts of a culture were on display for leisurely inspection. It is interesting to realize that some of the stalls were occupied by philosophers. A leisure occupation of those who could afford the wares was that of student. The school of Plato and later the school of Aristotle arose in much this same manner. Students came to dialogue with philosophers. "Employment of leisure" for schools has an honorable tradition.

Unfortunately, we have departed from that tradition. Today, school (the school model) means something totally foreign to that ancient tradition. The school model suggests not only the imparting of knowledge to students, but also inculcating or indoctrinating students. I suspect that most religious educators have uneasiness about the so-called school model. However, most ways of interpreting "schooling" today are still far removed from "employment of leisure." Yet, I would like to focus on "employment of leisure" in this chapter. In other words, I want to shift your attention away from ordinary pathways into new pathways. Take another look at church school!

John Westerhoff says to eliminate Sunday School.[1] Gabriel Moran says to forget parochial schools and concentrate on adult education.[2] The Gobels say to totally rearrange priorities in church.[3] From all sides, religious educators tell us what is wrong and, at a general level, what we must do about it. Revolutionary? Yes, I think so. In a sense, I agree with these revolutionaries. However, I do not necessarily agree with their means.

The Agora with its Stoa was introduced purposively. "Employment of leisure" was introduced purposively. The revolution (our present situation) was introduced purposively. My challenge now is to pull these three introductions together for you. I can do it from the orientation of attitude education.

THE STOA

The philosopher, or teacher, had a stall which opened out onto the spacious colonnade. Classes could be held outside at the base of a column in the sunshine, in the colonnade itself, or in the stall in inclement weather. The atmosphere of space, beauty, and simplicity made an excellent climate for the learner. Informality and a personal relationship between teacher and learner prevailed. Chairs and desks in aisles with the teacher on a podium at the head of the class were unheard of. The Stoa atmosphere suggests an atmosphere necessary for attitude education. Attitudes are not taught according to schedule. Attitudes are taught in "teachable moments." A story parents tell in order to stimulate a new behavior cannot be rigidly scheduled. Tantrums, sickness, or exhaustion must be circumvented. There is an informality in attitude education which is not served by our modern image of schooling. The Stoa schools provided an atmosphere which is more helpful. I am not saying that we should tear down our church schools and build Stoas. I am suggesting that you should pay attention to atmosphere and consider loosening up schedules, planned curriculum, and other rigidities which interfere with an atmosphere for attitude education.

Employment of Leisure

Greek learners went to school to employ their leisure. The individual learners were present under their own volition. They paid the teacher to be accessible to them. The British tutorial system and our informal seminars are the closest today to such use of leisure. Greek learners were motivated to learn at their leisure. If teachers were not meeting the learners' needs for learning, the learners were free to leave and choose other teachers in the Stoa. The result was a happy match between teacher and learner.

Attitude education, as I have presented it, has much in common with the concept of employment of leisure. Children make the decision to try new behaviors or responses at their own leisure. Attitudes are learned gradually and leisurely.

I believe that religious educators can benefit from establishing a more leisurely atmosphere in church schools.

Revolution

A revolution is an extensive radical change. From the orientation of attitude education, any changes cannot be sudden. Attitudes are learned gradually. Changes in religious education come more from evolution than from revolution. The changes I propose for a leisurely atmosphere in church schools will not come overnight. Changes in church school and in church worship depend upon changes in the attitudes of adults in the community. Adult attitude education must proceed step by step. The methodology presented for preschool children can work as well with adults: research, uniqueness, assessment, step by step, goal setting, building on strengths, stimulus, and reinforcement. You need not impose attitude education upon adults. You can cooperate with them in their own personal growth and education. Your church school teachers might be a good place to start. That is your most direct influence on changing gradually the atmosphere in your church school. However, you must also have the support of the minister, church officers, and, ultimately, the congregation.

A LOVING, LEISURELY ATMOSPHERE AND RELIGIOUS EDUCATION

Attitude education at its best demands a leisurely atmosphere. A leisurely atmosphere for religious attitude education also demands a loving, understanding community. Community participants at all age levels need religious attitude education. Preschool children need religious attitude education exclusively. Elementary school children begin to require information. Youth and adults require a great deal of information. I submit that information is important but ultimately the information must contribute to attitude formation if it is to affect behavior. Religious education which ignores the formation of attitudes is sadly missing the point. Again, I repeat, information is important, but only as it contributes to the formation of religious attitudes.

This chapter is on church school. I am proposing a loving, leisurely atmosphere for church school. However, I do not think that the bulk of religious education occurs in church schools, not even in the most loving and most leisurely of church schools. Religious education also occurs in families, in worship services, at church social functions, and at church meetings. Religious education occurs everywhere within the Christian community.

If religious education occurs throughout the Christian community, what unique part of religious education belongs to the church school? I do not support abolishing church schools. Yet I think that a distinct portion of religious education which is the responsibility of the church school can be clarified. I have suggested that learners learn love attitudes in community, wherever there is community. I have further suggested that learners learn faith attitudes in church worship. Now, I am proposing that the church school's contribution is providing a locus for the learning of *hope* attitudes.

The following Venn Diagram is a visual demonstration of loci and emphases which I envision.

This diagram makes the following assumptions:

1. Love as expressed in the loving community of the church is all encompassing. A church without love is a noisy gong or a clanging cymbal.
2. Faith as expressed in the church worship service is within the loving community.
3. Hope as expressed in church school is also within the loving community.
4. Within the loving community, faith and hope are distinct, yet they overlap.
5. Faith includes a portion of hope.
6. Hope includes a portion of faith.
7. Both faith and hope involve love and exist because of the loving community.

HOPE AND THE CHURCH SCHOOL

Now that I have (1) directed you toward perceiving religious education as concerned with *much* more than the church school and (2) I hope helped you to perceive of possibilities for providing a loving, leisurely atmosphere in your church school, I will proceed to focus on church school more specifically. Why hope for the church school? I gave you my definition of hope in chapter 5. It was two-pronged:

1. Reliance on the Kingdom of God now and hereafter;
2. Trust in the potential for obtaining greater knowledge and understanding of the unknown.

Reliance and trust suggest the intersection of faith and hope within love. However, the rest of the statements in (1) and (2) above suggest a distinctness about hope. "Hereafter" in (1) and "potential" in (2) suggest a future orientation of hope. "Obtaining greater knowledge and understanding" suggests the necessity of ever-expanding gathering of information. Preparations for dealing with the present and the future constitute hope. Schooling is a hopeful enterprise. Even today schooling is hoping. Teachers hope the learners will learn. The learners hope they will be provided with something to learn. On the other hand, hope is an attitude. Information learning contributes to an attitude of hope. The information, in and of itself, is not the whole of religious education. The church school should provide access to information, but the ultimate goal of the church school is hope, an attitude. Some religious educators will have to think long and hard about what I have said about community, worship, church school, and love, faith, and hope. I have rearranged some previous assumptions, but I have not revolutionized. I hope I have clarified some areas in need of theoretical clarification.

HOPE AND THE PRESCHOOL CHILD

The two educational goals for preschoolers were:

1. A positive attitude toward life;
2. A joyful attitude toward learning.

These two educational goals were derived from the initial definition of hope. The definition applies to mature Christians. The educational goals apply to that which is realistically possible for preschool children to learn. They are both goals that are filled with hope. If your church school can achieve these goals with preschool children, those children will be well prepared in foundational attitudes to face the challenges of life's transitions and crises.

EDUCATIONAL GOALS AND THE CHURCH SCHOOL

Much of what I will have to say from this point on has reference to the preschool level. However, many of my suggestions will certainly have implications for elementary school children in the church school. I will leave those implications up to you for your interpretation. I will do a better job if I retain my blinders for preschool religious education where dealing with headwaters is relatively clear.

1. A Positive Outlook on Life

One of the uplifting experiences for adults in the church community is the cheerfulness of some of the little children. Adults have a responsibility for the preschoolers.

The cheerfulness must be nurtured in a Christian community. This is mainly the job of adults, although qualified teenagers can play a very meaningful role. There are places in your community where you can enlist the help of loving, warm, patient, and understanding youth and adults. There are Crib Rooms or Play Rooms for infants and toddlers during church worship. (Of course, I am totally against the title of "Cry Room.") There are nursery classes and kindergarten classes. From what I have already written, I think you have predicted my suggestions for church school:

1. Bible stories should be carefully monitored so that children receive positive input on God and Jesus.
2. Schedules, curriculum, or any sort of rigidity should be very much relaxed.
3. Opportunities for joining in congregational worship should be encouraged depending on the children and on the situation.
4. Parents should be encouraged to work closely with teachers so that the needs of individual children are met.
5. Last, but of course not least, teachers should know how to go about attitude education.

I will not insult your intelligence at this point by reviewing all that has already been said on these matters. I will push on. You can review as you so desire.

However, if you review, look at the section on "A Positive Outlook on Life" in chapter 5. In that chapter, I attempted to call to your attention, by describing developmental levels, the importance to children of "fears" and "frustrations."

Now that the church school is specifically addressed, it is worthwhile to consider the hindrances of fears and frustrations to a positive outlook on life. How can church school teachers interact with preschool children so that problems of fears and frustrations can be prevented or at least diminished, during the formative years? If you think that these problems should be prevented during these preschool years, I agree. If you think they are completely unpreventable, you are not as idealistic that I am. If you think that there is no hope, I say that without hope there is no church school and, realistically, you may be out of a job.

There is hope. The methodology of attitude education gives you a tool to use in church school and elsewhere.

Fears

Initially, fears are caused by sudden, unfamiliar occurrences. A fear reaction is learned just as any other response is learned, by the bonding of a stimulus and a response. Thus, in your church school, introduce a leisurely atmosphere and limit sudden, unfamiliar occurrences. Stay with a leisurely routine particularly with children at the Toddler developmental level. Be sure that physical reassurances are available to toddlers. Be sure that simple explanations about fears are available to runabouts and on beyonds.

If these measures do not work and children are still full of fear, do not hesitate to summon the parents, particularly if the child is a toddler. The parents must make the decision about whether or not a child benefits from staying in church school.

Frustrations

A leisurely atmosphere must be an atmosphere in which frustrations are kept at a minimum. Generally speaking, when the developmental level of children is ignored, frustrations are bound to occur. Children get frustrated when too much is expected of them. They also get frustrated and bored when they are underchallenged. Frustrations can be avoided by paying attention to developmental levels. Match the children and the situation.

2. A Joyful Attitude toward Learning

This educational goal is closely related to a positive attitude toward life. Children who are happy about learning are children with a good chance of having a positive attitude toward life. Conversely, children who have unhappy experiences with learning are not likely to have a positive attitude toward life.

Fears and frustrations are reasons for unhappy learning experiences. Failure and "put-downs" also cause unhappy learning experiences. Make sure these negative outcomes do not occur in your church school. Children learn best from their successes. Failures should be ignored. Build on strengths in a loving, leisurely atmosphere.

Purposiveness, Persistence, and Creativity

Purposiveness, persistence, and creativity are the keys to encouraging a joyful attitude toward learning. You will remember from chapter 5 that these traits are not observed until the Runabout and On Beyond levels of development. Infants and Toddlers occasionally show behaviors suggesting these traits. All such behaviors should be encouraged.

The reason I say that purposiveness, persistence, and creativity are keys for joyful learning is that each can be used as a basis for the criteria you hope to meet in your church school. Put on your glasses tinted with purposiveness and observe your church school.

   a. Are the children encouraged for purposeful behavior?
   b. Are opportunities available to the children to practice skills for a purpose?
   c. Do the more mature children engage in work which they recognize as preparing themselves for anticipated events?

Now, put on your glasses tinted with persistence and observe your church school.

   a. Are the children encouraged for persistence?
   b. Are there opportunities for children to work on projects without interruptions?
   c. Can the more mature children begin to relate separate components in a complex task to the completed, whole task?

Finally, put on your creativity glasses.

   a. Are imagination and creativity reinforced?
   b. Are there opportunities for make-believe play, for storytelling, for music, painting, coloring, drawing, acting, dancing, singing?
   c. Are the more mature children helped with distinctions between make-believe and real?

If you can honestly answer "yes" to all those questions, I daresay the children are having fun learning and are developing a joyful attitude toward learning. Also, I daresay, there is a loving, leisurely atmosphere in your church school and an atmosphere of hope.

PARENTS AND THE CHURCH SCHOOL

In the previous two chapters, I closed each chapter by focusing again on parents. I will do the same thing for this chapter, but with a new twist. Previously, I have closed with a section on how parents can use the church as a resource in the attitude education of their children. I certainly hope your church school can *use* parents. I mean this quite seriously.

You can have a lovely church school with the correct color of paint on the walls, the correct equipment in each classroom, with loving, warm teachers, and with a leisurely, flexible schedule. Nevertheless, if your church school does not have parents, something is seriously wrong. If the parents' responsibility is no more than that of a chauffeur who drops off and picks up children, the religious education of those children is sadly lacking in essentials.

The primary locus of religious education for preschool children is in the home. The primary responsibility for religious education of preschool children belongs to the parents. They need your help in carrying out their responsibility. It is a seven-days-a-week task. They need all the resources their church can provide. The responsibility of church school is secondary. The responsibility of the church as community is secondary. That is not to say that the church as community is not important; it is. However, without religious education taking place in the homes, the community influence does not have much of a chance.

The church school ideally should supplement and complement what parents can do at home. This calls for close cooperation between teachers and parents. All the pieces must fit together to make religious education for preschoolers beneficial. Yes, I know I am challenging you to a delicate and daring game of chess. However, with the methodology of attitude education, I hope I have given you some instructions for playing the game.

Your chess set consists of the minister or priest, the church officers, committee members, teachers (I hope all the adults in the congregation belong to one of those categories), youth and children. You must decide upon who are kings, queens, bishops, knights, castles, and pawns. Set your priorities and play the game, supplementing and complementing according to your priorities.

The game I play is research. I do come out of my ivory tower often enough to appreciate the game you must play. I do appreciate the problems encountered by those of you on the firing line. However, I believe that the principles of attitude education which I have outlined can help you in your ministry. In education there is always hope. I have a few remaining suggestions which I make in order to encourage (reinforce) your hope. I will state them as my beliefs.

1. I believe that teachers deserve the assistance of a teacher's aide at each and every class session. Furthermore, I believe that the teacher's aides should be the parents of the children in the class. Parents should participate at least once a month.

   a. I do not agree with many systems where teachers are enlisted quarterly or semi-annually. When their stint is done, they are free. Preschool children need consistency. Teacher aides (parents) can help alleviate the closed-off feelings of teachers.

   b. Children benefit by witnessing their parents' active participation in church school. Parents are children's models in the early years. Parents should be present during the years of transfer to other authority figures during the later preschool years.

2. I believe that the church school must both supplement and complement the religious education taking place in the home. I realize that this calls for enormous coordination and close cooperation between teachers and parents, but it is worth it for the children.

   a. In your contacts with parents, you do have the role of mediator.
   b. In your contacts with teachers, you also have a mediator's role.
   c. Can you play the chess game here? Can you support what should be taking place in homes and also support what is going on in the church school? I'm sure you can figure out how to play this exciting game.

3. I believe that decisions about what takes place in church school are the joint responsibility of teachers and parents (guided by you as Director of Religious Education).

4. Finally, I believe that the director of religious education has the right to set standards for the teachers and the parents in the church school and to expect those standards to be met.

   a. Teachers should be certified to teach as a result of training in attitude education.
   b. The DRE and parents should have a contractual relationship for every pupil. Contracts should specify the responsibilities of the parents in their home teaching and in their participation in church school duties.

The task of the professional religious educator is not for the fainthearted. Bold measures are required in order for your church school to become the place of hope that it potentially can become. Set your sights high. Create the teamwork you need between parents, teachers, and the rest of the congregation. Together create a loving, leisurely atmosphere in your church school so that the children can learn attitudes of hope. Coordinate your church school with church worship so that the children learn attitudes of faith. Relate the activities of your church school with all the activities in your church community so that the children can learn attitudes of love.

Chapter 14

The Potential
of Religious Education

Now I am going to take off my preschool blinders and take another look at where you and I have been. Some interesting things have happened, at least as far as I am concerned. You see, I did not know that I would wind up where I have. I began by exploring the headwaters of religious education. My original plan was to end the book with chapter 8. I gave you the educational goals, the eight principles of attitude education, and the down-to-earth applications in the illustrations. Essentially, I was introducing you to a methodology of attitude education informed by psychological theory. I was willing to call it quits at that point. My publisher wanted more. He told me to "cover the waterfront."

At first, I was flabbergasted. You see, I approach talking to religious educators with some trepidation because of natural hesitancies whenever professionals from differing disciplines talk to one another. On the other hand, I am devoted to religious education and believe that psychologists can help. I am encouraged by the current trend of religious educators' using psychology to their own advantage. I am a psychologist ready and willing to help religious educators. My hope is that I have helped you to take a fresh look at religious education.

Originally, I thought of writing more chapters as one more chore. Yet, how glad I am now that I plunged into the task. I did not know how the journey would end. I did know that the journey could be taken. Journeys are explorations as one covers new ground. I have made many discoveries along the way. It has been an exciting trip for me. Perhaps it has been a perplexing, frustrating trip for you.

I started the journey with the premise that religious education for preschool children is attitude education. The concept of education for preoperational children must be translated into attitude education. There is no other rational way. Attitude education encompasses the affective and the cognitive. Attitude education encompasses nurture and information giving. Attitude education also reorients. In the shallow headwaters, attitude education can be readily appreciated as the only possible beginnings of religious education.

Thus, with the orientation of attitude education, one begins to view religious education in a different light. As I review our journey, I begin to realize some of the perplexities I have challenged you with. For example, I ended the book with church school. Perhaps in a book for religious educators, you expected me to *begin* with church school. An attitude education orientation does not lead in that direction. Church school is low on the list of priorities in attitude education. The family comes first. Therefore, I implore you to reorganize your priorities in order to help you reconsider your ministry to parents. Religious education is much broader than the church school. You have a responsibility to parents.

In fact, if you overlook parents, two results may occur. Either you will be remarkably lucky and have outstanding parents who just naturally educate their children in attitudes, or you will have ordinary parents and religious education will go on as always without anyone being very enthusiastic. However, if you go about educating parents, then you will begin to see remarkable things happening in your church school. If you will train your teachers in attitude education, further remarkable things will happen in your church school.

With trained parents and teachers working together so that attitude education is high priority in church school, the place that information holds in a curriculum will become obvious. The children will show you when they are eager for information because they have an attitude of hope and an attitude that learning facts is a joy. I suspect that elementary school children require a good bit of information. I suspect that adolescents require even more information. The formation of teenagers' attitudes should incorporate facts and information. They should hope to find information in church school if they have foundational attitudes from childhood which are hopeful.

Once you have trained parents and teachers, you can turn your attention to church worship. If the priest or minister is not on your side with an orientation to attitude education you have a serious problem. Subtle education is called for, along with your patience, persistence, and large doses of faith, hope, and love.

When the time is right, discuss church worship with the priest or minister. Plan gradual changes in the worship service so that children can participate and can learn by doing faith. Include parents and teachers in the planning so that a team is involved. As progress is made, the entire congregation will be part of the team. That is the time when your church will truly become a loving community.

As attitude education includes all of the parish, you will see changes in church suppers, stewardship drives, church fairs, all of the church's activities. Your church will be the best possible resource for parents and their children. It will be a place for children to learn love by being loved and by loving others.

I see great potential for religious education. The starting point is the parents of preschoolers. They must learn how to teach attitudes to their children. If parents can teach children the foundational attitudes for mature religious attitudes, you are making great progress. If you can support parents and at the same time train teachers and other adults in the methodology of attitude education, you will make further strides toward gradually making religious education of benefit to all. When faith, hope, and love are happening in your church, religious education is happening. It can be done.

"Despite our deficiencies, still, in our churches at their best, lives are transformed, character is built, courage is renewed, faith is strengthened, ideals of personal and social conduct which else would die are kept alive. Public-spirited devotion is engendered, and God's kingdom of righteousness on earth is made a living hope."[1] I believe that Fosdick was speaking about the results of attitude education in our church communities at their best.

APPENDICES

Notes

CHAPTER 1

1. I will be using the term, "mature," not solely in a psychological sense, but in its traditional sense throughout this book. A good synonym is "well-developed." A mature Christian is a person with well-developed religious attitudes, judgments, and behavior. A mature preschooler is one with well-developed attitudes, judgments, and behavior for that developmental level, although *I* would call those attitudes, judgments, and behavior *pre*religious.

2. Although Dr. Goldman labeled preschool children as prereligious in "Religious Thinking from Childhood to Adolescence" (Routledge and Kegan Paul, London, 1964), he went to some length to describe possibilities for religious education for prereligious children in "Readiness for Religion" (London: Routledge and Kegan Paul, 1965).

3. The well-known developmental theory of emotions of K. M. B. Bridges is well explained by Don C. Dinkmeyer in "Child Development: the Emerging Self" (Englewood Cliffs, New Jersey: Prentice-Hall, Inc., 1965).

4. For further information about the three domains, see: Benjamin S. Bloom (ed.), "Taxonomy of Educational Objectives, Handbook I: Cognitive Domain; David R. Krathwohl, Benjamin S. Bloom and Bertram B. Masia, "Taxonomy of Educational Objectives, Handbook II: Affective Domain," and Anita J. Harrow, "A Taxonomy of the Psychomotor Domain." All of these books were published by David McKay Company, New York.

The dates are 1956, 1964, and 1972 respectively. All authors subscribe to a dynamic interaction among domains.

5. See Milton Rokeach, *Beliefs, Attitudes, and Values* (San Francisco: Jossey-Bass, Inc., 1970), p. 132.

6. Milton Rokeach, *The Open and Closed Mind* (New York: Basic Books, 1960).

7. Milton Rokeach, *The Nature of Human Values* (New York: The Free Press, 1973).

8. An overview of the subject can be found in Sidney B. Simon, Leland W. Howe, and Howard Kirschenbaum, *Values Clarification* (New York: Hart, 1972). Many of the techniques are useful with children particularly when used for religious purposes.

CHAPTER 2

1. Ellis C. Nelson, *Where Faith Begins* (Richmond: John Knox, 1967). Gabriel Moran, *Vision and Tactics: Toward an Adult Church* (New York: Herder and Herder, 1968).

2. John Westerhoff, *Values for Tomorrow's Children: An Alternative Future for Education in the Church* (Philadelphia: Pilgrim Press, 1970).

3. James Michael Lee, *The Flow of Religious Instruction: A Social Science Approach* (Birmingham, Alabama: Religious Education Press, 1973).

4. References for other books on attitude education can be found in Appendix B where references are annotated.

CHAPTER 3

1. See Horace B. English and Ava Champney English, *A Comprehensive Dictionary of Psychological and Psychoanalytical Terms* (New York: David McKay Company, 1962).

2. A common belief is that deprivations during the early years are permanently damaging for the rest of life. Ann M. Clarke and A. D. B. Clarke assert convincingly that this belief is a myth

(*Early Experience: Myth and Evidence* [New York: The Free Press, 1976]). Nonetheless, if little children learn the foundations for faith, hope, and love, they will have a richer start in their religious education.

3. James Michael Lee, *The Flow of Religious Instruction: A Social Science Approach* (Birmingham, Alabama: Religious Education Press, 1973), pp. 116–118.

4. See J. Bowlby, *Maternal Care and Mental Health* (Geneva: World Health Organization) for a review of research on deprivation during infancy.

5. B. F. Skinner, *Beyond Freedom and Dignity* (New York: Knopf, 1971).

6. "Uniqueness" is a difficult concept for an educator to entertain. A unique learner is different from every other learner! What can a teacher do with a class of twenty unique learners? While it is true that every learner is unique, it is also true that, developmentally, learners have more in common than they have just to themselves. Thus, the term, "uniqueness," should not be avoided. A psychometrician of Leona Tyler's stature is bold enough to find uniqueness helpful. (Leona E. Tyler, *Individuality: Human Possibilities and Personal Choice in the Psychological Development of Men and Women* (San Francisco: Jossey-Bass, 1978.) Thus, I am also going to use the term. If it would be helpful to you to substitute "individuality," go ahead and do so. Parents will not have the difficulty that educators have with uniqueness. Most parents agree that their children are unique, as indeed they are.

7. A sensitive treatment of this subject can be found in: Johanna Klink, *Your Child and Religion* (Richmond, Virginia: John Knox Press, 1972).

CHAPTER 4

1. Ernest M. Ligon, *The Psychology of Christian Personality* (New York: Macmillan, 1946).

2. Ernest M. Ligon, *Their Future is Now* (New York: Macmillan, 1959).

3. A condensation of CRP's Research Curriculum can be found in: Herman Williams and Ella Greene, *Attitude Education: A Research Curriculum* (Schenectady, N.Y.: Character Research Press, 1975).

CHAPTER 5

1. Very young children are hedonistic, as well they may be. Egocentricity is the explanation. Unless and until children can appreciate other persons as distinct from self, the self is all there is to please.

2. Little children are frustrated whenever the gratification of their desires is delayed. They want what they want when they want it—not later. This is a normal phase for egocentric toddlers. Other prominent frustrations are interferences with their budding independence.

3. Reflex actions in response to loud noises or falling are random behaviors as a result of surprise by an unfamiliar stimulus. Fear, per se, is not differentiated until about six months of age.

4. I have noticed in CRP protocols a tendency of parents to deny their children's fantasy stage of development. Fantasy is a right of children which should be celebrated. See Lucie W. Barber, *Realistic Parenting* (St. Meinrad, Indiana: Abbey Press, 1980), for further discussion.

CHAPTER 6

1. Stories as stimuli in attitude education is dealt with in detail in: Lucie W. Barber, *When Parents Tell Stories* (St. Meinrad, Indiana: Abbey Press, 1980).

CHAPTER 7

1. One of the most concise sources for a review of learning theory is B. R. Bugelski, *The Psychology of Learning Applied to Teaching* (New York: Bobbs-Merrill Co., Inc., 1964).

2. In the lists of stimuli, I use the term *stimulus* in its broadest sense: "Any phenomenon, object, aspect of an object, or event, however conceived or described, which modifies behavior by eliciting activity in a sense organ," English and English, *A Comprehensive Dictionary of Psychological and Psychoanalytic Terms* (New York: David McKay, 1962). Thus, stories and swimming pools are stimuli.

3. "Intrinsic stimuli" is a coined term as is "intrinsic reinforcer." My purpose in introducing these terms will become clearer in chapter 8.

4. Parents contributed written reports to the Character Research Project from 1967 to 1971. These were parents of children from birth to thirty months of age who were enrolled in the "Infancy Design." The book, *Let Me Introduce My Self,* by Ligon, Barber, and Williams (Schenectady, N.Y.: Character Research Press, 1976) was the result of the Infancy Design, as was the book, *Celebrating the Second Year of Life*, by Barber (Birmingham, Alabama: Religious Education Press, 1979). The quotes on pages 67–80 are my paraphrasing as a result of extensive knowledge of that body of data.

5. When parents reinforce children's responses, the assumption is clear that a parental behavior is involved. In this example, "signs of my pleasure" assumes that the signs are behaviors portraying pleasure such as smiles or verbalizations about the weather. In succeeding illustrations parents write of awe, enthusiasm, and praise as reinforcers. Again, the assumption is made that awe, enthusiasm, and praise are inferred because of some behavior.

CHAPTER 8

1. B. F. Skinner, *Beyond Freedom and Dignity* (New York: Knopf, 1971).

2. Intrinsic conditioning is a coined term. It implies a self-directed learner who self-stimulates and self-reinforces. This is similar to an andragogue. Andragogy was introduced in this

country by Malcolm Knowles. See *Self-Directed Learning: A Guide for Learners and Teachers* (New York: Association Press, 1975). Maurice Gibbons in Canada is also engaged in self-education. See Gibbons et al., "Toward a Theory of Self-Directed Learning: A Study of Experts Without Formal Training," *Journal of Humanistic Psychology* 20, No. 2 (Spring, 1980).

CHAPTER 9

1. With James Michael Lee, I would like to "despookify" religious education. However, I will not take "magic" out of what religious educators must understand about preschool children. For those of us who are beyond preoperational thinking, I believe that "magic" helps us to understand the little children. From the past come the words of Evelyn Underhill: ". . . Magic is merely a system whereby the self tries to assuage its transcendental curiosity by extending the activities of the will beyond their usual limits" (Evelyn Underhill, *Mysticism: A Study in the Nature and Development of Man's Spiritual Consciousness* [London: Methuen and Co., Ltd., 1911]). Children in their preoperational thinking need the power of magic in order to assimilate their environment which to them yet makes little sense. In Underhill's terms, they want to "touch the button" and magic will do the rest. Interestingly, Piaget describes the magic stage of preoperational thinkers in much the same way (Jean Piaget, *The Child's Conception of Physical Causality* (Paterson, N.J.: Littlefield, Adams and Company, 1960). His animism stage is characterized by the child in power, able to push the button in order to obtain immediate answers that self-satisfy for the moment.

2. The quotes in this paragraph are taken, with permission, from *Children's Religious Concepts* (Union College Character Research Project, Schenectady, New York, 1959).

3. Jerome Berryman is well-known for his work with children and parables. His language differs from mine, but I would say that he and I generally agree. See his article, "Being in Parables with Children," *Religious Education* 74, No. 3 (May–June, 1979).

4. Iris Cully has a sensitive treatment of using the Bible with children in *Christian Child Development* (San Francisco: Harper and Row, 1979). She believes in adjusting Bible stories to individual children as long as one is faithful to the meaning of scripture.

CHAPTER 10

1. The following books by Jerome S. Bruner are helpful concerning the ways children learn mathematics: *On Knowing: Essays for the Left Hand* (New York: Atheneum, 1965); and *Toward a Theory of Instruction* (Cambridge, Massachusetts: Belknap Press, 1966).

CHAPTER 11

1. John Westerhoff specifies four criteria for church communities, one of which is "the presence and interaction of three generations." *Will Our Children Have Faith?* (New York: Seabury Press, 1976).

2. Recorded cases of remarkable recoveries from child abuse can be found in Ann M. Clarke and A. D. B. Clarke, *Early Experience: Myth and Evidence* (New York: The Free Press, 1976).

3. Erik Erikson, *Childhood and Society* (New York: Norton 1950). Abraham Maslow, *Motivation and Personality* (New York: Harper, 1954.

CHAPTER 12

1. Fowler has drawn our attention to faith as a verb. James Fowler and Sam Keen, *Life Maps: Conversations on the Journey of Faith* (Waco, Texas: Word Books, 1979).

2. After my father's death, Westminster Press published *Children's Sermons,* by Kenneth B. Welles. Unfortunately, the book is out of print now.

3. At least three sources supplied me with ideas: 1. Dennis C. Benson and Stan J. Steward, *The Ministry of the Child* (Nashville, Tennessee: Abingdon, 1979). 2. A. Roger Gobbel and Gertrude G. Gobbel, "Children and Worship," *Religious Education* 74, No. 6 (1979). 3. John Westerhoff, *Will Our Children Have Faith?* (New York: Seabury Press, 1976).

4. The quotes on this page are taken, with permission, from *Children's Religious Concepts* (Union College Character Research Project, Schenectady, New York, 1959).

CHAPTER 13

1. John Westerhoff, *Values for Tomorrow's Children* (Philadelphia, Pennsylvania: Pilgrim Press, 1970).

2. Gabriel Moran, *Vision and Tactics* (New York: Herder and Herder, 1968).

3. A. Rodger Gobbel and Gertrude G. Gobbel, "Children and Worship," *Religious Education*, 74, No. 6 (1979).

CHAPTER 14

1. Harry Emerson Fosdick, *A Faith for Tough Times* (New York: Harper and Brothers, 1952).

Additional Resources

RESOURCES FOR PARENTS

In addition to this book, there are four other resources which come out of the background research of the Union College Character Research Project:

1. *Let Me Introduce My Self.* E. M. Ligon, L. W. Barber, and H. J. Williams. Schenectady, New York: Character Research Press, 1976.

   At first glance, parents flipping through this book get the impression of a diary, plus some text and some delightful cartoons of infants. That is correct. However, the book is actually a carefully designed educational system for parents of children, newborns through thirty months of age. The text is in the words of the baby, communicating needs and wants to parents. The diary sections even further focus the parents' attention on their unique, communicating children.

   Based on developmental levels, the attitudes involved in this book address purposiveness, social effectiveness, and an emerging value system.

   Broadman Press has published this same book for South-

---

*Many of the descriptions of books for parents are taken, with permission, from an essay review in *Religious Education:* Lucie W. Barber, "Parents and Children: The First Years of Life," *Religious Education* 75, No. 1 (January–February, 1980).

ern Baptists under the title, *Looking At Me.* The only difference is the addition of an introduction by C. Sybil Waldrop which emphasizes the religious dimensions involved. Panamedia Press has also published the section covering the first twelve months under the title, *If You Only Knew What Your Baby Is Thinking.*

2. *Celebrating the Second Year of Life: A Parent's Guide to a Happy Child.* Lucie W. Barber. Birmingham, Alabama: Religious Education Press, 1979.

Attitude education as you have been reading about it in the present book is spelled out for parents in this book. The eight principles are there, but not in the language you have read. Only the Toddler level is discussed. However, that level is further refined in a step-by-step process. Parents assess their children and then are referred to specific sections explaining exactly what they can do with and for their children.

The attitudes involved are (1) joy of learning, (2) self-confidence and independence, (3) positive self-image, (4) associating with others happily, and (5) trust and faith that the environment is predictable. I trust these sound familiar.

3. *Parents' Packet for the Barber Scales of Self-Regard for Preschool Children.* Lucie W. Barber and the research staff of the Union College Character Research Project. Schenectady, New York: Character Research Press, 1975.

The packet contains (1) a parents' guide, (2) seven scales of self-regard, and (3) a profile. The parents' guide is essentially a record-keeping device for parents to note uniqueness and record observations. The seven scales of self-regard are "Purposeful Learning of Skills," "Completing Tasks," "Coping with Fears," "Children's Responses to Requests," "Dealing with Frustrations," "Socially Acceptable Behavior," and "Developing Imagination in Play." Again, I trust these titles sound familiar to you. Each represents a self-environment interaction derived from a theoretical model of integrated personality. The profile provides parents who have rated their children on the seven scales an opportunity to plot a seven-point profile at a point in time for their children.

4. *Realistic Parenting.* Lucie W. Barber, John H. Peatling, John Hiltz, and Louise Marie Skoch. St. Meinrad, Indiana: Abbey Press, 1980.

   The Parents' Packet for the Barber Scales of Self-Regard for Preschool Children was the basis for a group program for parenting education. *Realistic Parenting* was successfully field-tested in conjunction with the Diocese of Toledo, Ohio. The program, now receiving nationwide attention, includes a leader's guide, a parent's workbook, and audio-visual supplements. More books from Abbey Press relating to parenting of preschoolers can be expected.

The next books are easy reading and short:

1. *When Your Child Needs a Hug.* Larry Losoncy. St. Meinrad, Indiana: Abbey Press, 1978.

   Emotional development during infancy, childhood, and adolescence is emphasized.

2. *When Your Child Learns to Choose.* Andrew D. Thompson. St. Meinrad, Indiana: Abbey Press, 1978.

   The moral development of children, birth through adolescence, is described. Christian parents are shown how they can help their children develop Christian values.

3. *When Parents Tell Stories.* Lucie W. Barber. St. Meinrad, Indiana: Abbey Press, 1980.

   The whys and hows of storytelling are emphasized. This is an attitude education primer for parents of preschoolers. A story, of course, is a stimulus.

There are other books for parents which are longer and more fully developed:

1. *Your Child's Self Esteem.* Dorothy C. Briggs. Garden City, New York: Doubleday and Co., Inc., Dolphin Books, 1975.

This book has been referenced by religious educators although religion per se is not dealt with. The author is a psychologist and educator. Her guidelines "for raising responsible, productive, happy children" are worth attention.

2. *Raising Children in a Difficult Time*. Benjamin Spock. New York: Norton and Company, Inc., 1974.

The high ideals of this favorite author are translated into parenting possibilities in modern times. There is even a complete section on attitudes, plus references to religion. While I do not entirely endorse Spock's approach to attitude education, there is a great deal of common sense in this book.

3. *Strong Family, Strong Child: The Art of Working Together to Develop a Healthy Child*. Barry Bricklin and Patricia Bricklin. New York: Delacorte Press, 1970.

The authors are child psychologists particularly interested in communication between family members.

4. *The Emerging Personality: Infancy Through Adolescence*. George E. Gardner, New York: Delacorte Press, 1970.

This book is written by a psychiatrist for parents and professionals, with emphasis on developmental tasks. Religion is barely touched upon; however, as supplementary reading for interested parents, the information is extensive and worthwhile.

I am well aware of the numerous books that are left out of any listing. My criteria for choosing the above four books were (1) emphasis on development, (2) thoroughness of treatment, and (3) practicality. These books have treated infancy through adolescence. You may want supplementary books more specifically aimed for parents of preschool children. The following books are concerned with either the first two and a half years or all five of the preschool years:

1. *Growing With Children*. Joseph and Laurie Braga. Englewood Cliffs, New Jersey: Prentice-Hall, Inc., 1974.

The authors are developmental psychologists. They explain the needs, capabilities and limitations of children in the preschool years. Their mission is to expose the concept of parents growing with their children.

2. *Survival Handbook for Preschool Mothers.* Helen Wheeler Smith. Chicago: Follett Publishing Company, 1977.

   This book is a regular smorgasbord of concrete suggestions. The style is light and the pace is rapid. Emphasis is on the child's self-esteem. The approach is positive. The author is also concerned about the well-being of mothers.

3. *Child Learning Through Child Play.* Ira Gordon. New York: St. Martin's Press, 1972.

   This is an attractive, easy to read book of games by a well-known authority in early childhood development. Parents are asked to research their child to determine what works best. Dr. Gordon does not use the term "research" however.

4. *Toddlers and Parents: A Declaration of Independence.* T. Berry Brazelton. New York: Delacorte Press, 1974.

   This well-known pediatrician writes to parents of children in the "terrible twos" stage. His compassion extends to both children and their parents.

5. *The Roots of Love: Helping Your Child Learn to Love in the First Three Years of Life.* Helene S. Arnstein. Indianapolis/New York: The Bobbs-Merrill Company, Inc., 1975.

   It is obvious from the title why I chose this book. Other reasons for choosing this book are a special emphasis on fathers and sections on marriage, prebirth, and birth.

RESOURCES FOR RELIGIOUS EDUCATORS

Here are a few texts on child development which can help you expand your knowledge:

1. *Child Development: The Emerging Self.* Don C. Dinkmeyer. Englewood Cliffs, New Jersey: Prentice-Hall, 1965.

2. *Child Development.* Elizabeth B. Hurlock. New York: McGraw-Hill, Inc., 1973.
3. *Child Psychology.* Arthur T. Jersild, Englewood Cliffs, New Jersey: Prentice-Hall, 1960.
4. *Child Psychology: Behavior and Development.* Donald C. Johnson and Gene R. Medinnus. New York: John Wiley and Sons, Inc., 1969.
5. *The Child and His Image.* Kaoru Yamamuto. Boston: Houghton Mifflin, 1972.

In this Appendix on Additional Resources, you may have wondered why there are so few authors who are religious educators. Did you know that according to one journalist's count there are about 15,000 books available to parents of infants and preschool children? Naturally, I have not read 15,000 books. What interested me was the comparison between the number of books available in the secular market and the number available in the religious market. To obtain a rough estimate, I checked the *Religious Education* book review sections, *The New Review of Books and Religion,* and several catalogs from the so-called "religious publishing houses." Admittedly, the search was not exhaustive. Even so, the hard fact was apparent: there are very few books of a religious nature available about parenting of infants and preschoolers which even approach a developmental stance. Jeanne Boggs, University of Maryland, did her doctoral dissertation on an analysis of 32 contemporary Christian child-rearing manuals. Two of her findings struck me particularly. (1) Very few of the manuals dealt with infancy and early childhood, and (2) behavioral science theory and research played only a secondary role. Thus, there are not many additional resources which supplement this book from the discipline of religious education. However, I would like to mention a few. The authors of the first two books are religious educators. The focus of these books is on children and what we can learn from children. I have repeatedly emphasized the importance of parents' researching their own children. These two books suggest observing and listening to children from a different viewpoint. Nevertheless, I believe they are worth your attention if you wish to broaden your interest in what religious educators can learn from children.

1. *Your Child and Religion.* Johanna Klink. Richmond, Virginia: John Knox Press, 1971.

    This book is the translation from Dutch of an immensely popular book in Europe. Your attention is drawn to the actual quotes from well-known authorities remembering their own childhood experience with religion. The author demonstrates exquisite sensitivity to the consequences of children's misinterpreting the outmoded hell-fire and damnation approach to religion. She adds convincing evidence for the validity of the positive approach: build on strengths.

2. *The Ministry of the Child.* Dennis C. Benson and Stan J. Stewart. Nashville, Tennessee: Abingdon, 1979.

    If you do not get carried away by the thought that children actually teach adults religion, this book can add to your sensitivity about what the presence of children can offer to a congregation.

The last three books are by religious educators who are attempting to put teachers and parents in touch with social scientists, particularly psychologists and to interpret for their readers what research results may mean in Christian education. I include these books because they relate to topics in this book. One of these books is about the life cycle. In reading chapter 8, you were aware of the importance I put on an orientation in religious education which incorporates a life-cycle approach. Also, these books refer to psychologists Jean Piaget, B. F. Skinner, Erik Erikson, Ronald Goldman, and others to whom I as a psychologist give concentrated attention in all of my work. On the other hand, I believe that as a child psychologist I must warn you that I consider these books noble attempts, but no more. I believe that it is time to bridge the gap between psychology and religious education to the benefit of both disciplines. I applaud Cully, Elias, and Losoncy for their efforts. They are not psychologists; they are primarily religious educators. Their interpretation of the research of psychologists is perhaps somewhat free (at best) or somewhat misinformed (at worst). However, they have made an important stride. My fond hope is that they will provide you with a stimulus to read their references yourselves so that you will be reinforced by the primary sources. You can learn from psychologists just as psychologists must learn from you.

1. *Christian Child Development.* Iris V. Cully. San Francisco: Harper and Row, 1979.

2. *Psychology and Religious Education.* John L. Elias. Bethlehem, Pennsylvania: Catechetical Communications, 1975.

3. *Religious Education and the Life Cycle.* Lawrence Losoncy. Bethlehem, Pennsylvania: Catechetical Communications, 1977.

The last two books which I wish to call to your attention are introductions to the work of Jean Piaget. I strongly believe that all responsible religious educators should be familiar with Piaget.

1. *Understanding Piaget: An Introduction to Children's Cognitive Development.* Mary Ann Spencer Pulaski. New York: Harper and Row, 1971.

2. *The Psychology of the Child.* Jean Piaget and Barbel Inhelder. New York: Basic Books, 1969.

Index of Names

Index of Subjects